FRANCE
The Final Days

From the authors of the *I Hate The French Official Handbook*, the *I Hate Europe Official Handbook* and *Saving Graces and other Poetic Gems* – a new and outrageous exposé of the F-place.

FRANCE
The Final Days

DENISE THATCHER

in collaboration with

MALCOLM SCOTT

with illustrations by

MARTIN BAKER

CARLTON

This book is dedicated to
my Mum, Morgan and the 2 M's Winebar.
With thanks to: the massively knowledgeable
Ian McLaren, Mel, Mark Buckingham, Quasimodo, Kid, Janet,
Ronnie Biggs, Simon, Mike & Helen, young Belinda, Irena,
Nigel Blundell and, as ever, Peter Kenworthy

THIS IS A CARLTON BOOK

Text copyright © 1998 Malcolm Scott
Design copyright © 1998 Carlton Books Limited

First Published in 1998 by
Carlton Books Limited
20 St Anne's Court
Wardour Street
London W1V 3AW

1 3 5 7 9 10 8 6 4 2

A CIP catalogue record for this book is available from the British Library.

ISBN 1 85868 594 X

Printed and bound in Great Britain

Contents

metamorphosis of the garlic

WARNING

This book is intended as a work of satire.
Do not on any account take seriously or rely upon
any of the facts or opinions contained within.
Failure by individuals to be amused at certain
passages in this book may be construed as evidence
of Gallic origin.

Introduction

Willy-nilly, Great Britain is moving closer to the Continent. As we sign up to the Social Chapter, as Eurofighter reaches for the sky and as Eurotunnel's debt mountain achieves Himalayan proportions, we find, like it or not, that our fate, our national destiny is ever more intimately bound up with those of people who live somewhere else.

In the vanguard of these non-subjects of the House of Windsor, dwelling in the Land of Gaul, are to be discovered a people we shall call the French. Their mission is to run the world from Paris, their role-model, a Corsican corporal.

Should they be allowed to succeed with their plans, Chanel No. 19 will gush from our public fountains and there will soon be a bidet in every bungalow. Tony Blair has wisely seen fit to take a rain-check on the inevitable catastrophe of monetary union, but do we really want to eat snail-flavoured crisps and see our cod and chips dipped in a garlic batter?

One thing we cannot afford is complacency and the present volume will, I fervently believe, do much to promote the moral re-armament of which we are so patently needful. Remember always that behind every Frenchman there squats a German.

Fakhreldine Samosa
Laudanum Mansions, Arnold Lane

Why Be Rude To The French?

The rivalry between France and England is an ancient and honourable one. It is founded on the fact that we are so close and yet so different.

We may tease and make fun of each other because we are of comparable status. We may not be equals, but at least we play in the same division.

Woe betide he or she who would make us guard our tongues or put away our pens when we are in mid-insult, save only if that which we are saying or writing is crass or unoriginal.

Let no blows be exchanged between us except at Twickenham and Le Parc des Princes.

P.S. If and when you feel that the situation over there is getting completely out of control, I'm sure we can arrange direct rule from Westminster.

The only good thing to come out of France is the Dover ferry!

14

10 First Class Reasons For Not Being Perhaps Best Pleased With The French

1. Letting smouldering lorries onto their end of Eurotunnel

2. Algeria

3. Not eating enough succulent British beef

4. Le Tunnel D'Alma

5. Jansenism

6. Folkestone

7. The World Cup ticket fiasco

8. Taking all our decent fish

9. Sending us their "apples"

10. Bernard Tapie

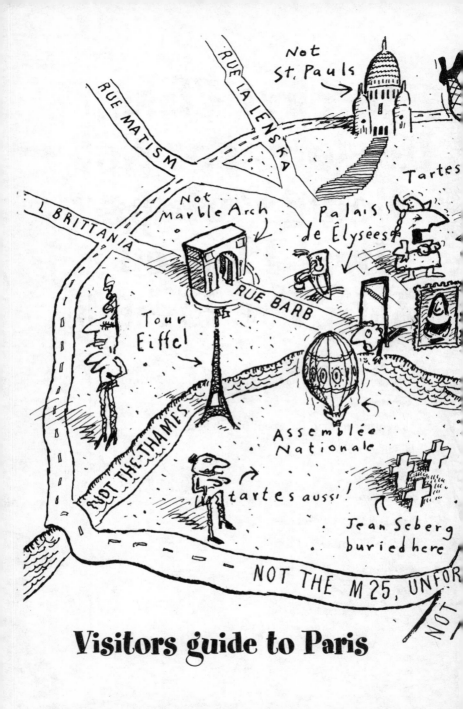

Visitors guide to Paris

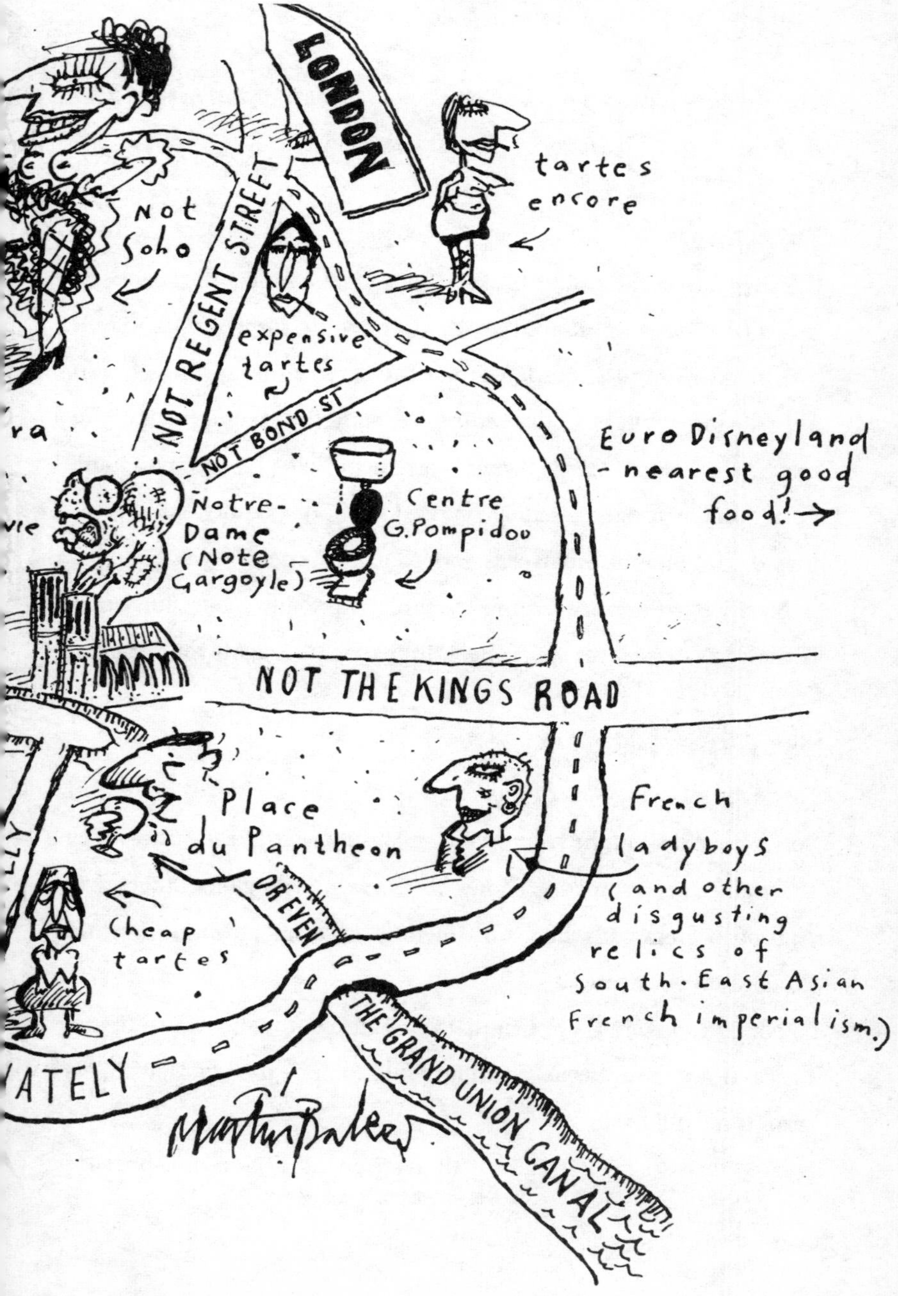
LONDON
tartes encore
Not Soho
NOT REGENT STREET
expensive tartes
NOT BOND ST
ra
Euro Disneyland - nearest good food! →
Notre-Dame (Note Gargoyle)
Centre G.Pompidou
vie
NOT THE KINGS ROAD
Place du Pantheon
French ladyboys (and other disgusting relics of South-East Asian French imperialism.)
LLY
OR EVEN
Cheap tartes
ATELY
THE GRAND UNION CANAL
Martin Baker

This guide is provided by the Greater Paris Tourist Authority to help make your stay all the more pleasant and gay.

Language

It is illegal to speak bad or broken French – the Académie Française levies very large fines, and has been known to imprison persistent offenders. You are permitted to use medieval Norman French, but only during daylight hours on the left bank. In an emergency, you may use the word "Merde" which can mean Hello, Please and Thank You. Foreign languages may be used without penalty, so long as they do not include any words derived from French.

Native Parisians are required to understand any major language. If they do not, please report them, in person, to the Mayor of Paris.

Transport

It is compulsory to carry dogs at all times on the Métro system. If you have not brought your own dog, simply wait at the entrance to the station until someone comes out carrying a dog of suitable size. Approach them with the usual greeting "Giva'sat", take the dog and proceed on your way.

Foreign visitors do not need to buy tickets for the Metro or the buses. If an inspector asks you for your "billet", merely reply, "This train is my billet, sir."

Taxi drivers in Paris are all trained as diplomats and are

inevitably polite. Part of their official duty is to change all kinds of foreign money and large bank notes. They should not be offered tips, as this impugns their professional standing.

Remember, pedestrians have the right of way on all roads. Just step off the pavement and watch all the drivers brake and wave you through.

Entertainment

There are a growing number of British-style pubs in Paris, which are trying to be as authentic as possible. When you go into one, please remember:

- Always order in English and pay in pounds.
- Always complain about the beer – it will either be too warm or too cold.
- The locals keep disguising the dart board as a table football machine – just prop it back up against the wall.
- Every seventh round you order is traditionally paid for by the landlord.
- Spitting and snuff-taking are encouraged – ask the barman for the snuff-box.
- Visiting bagpipers should always play immediately they enter the pub to scare away evil spirits.

Visitors to the Eiffel Tower should remember to take a bottle of wine with them. It is considered good luck to drink the wine on the top balcony, and then throw the empty bottle into the Seine.

You should note that anyone staying in Paris for less than 10 days is allowed to jump the queue at the Louvre and Orsay museums. Flautists are banned from the pyramid at the Louvre for obvious reasons.

Free parties for visitors are held at the British Embassy on Tuesdays (from 9pm), the Elysée Palace on Thursdays (from 8.30pm, please use the side door) and the National Assembly on Saturdays (from 8pm, casual dress). Invitations are not required, and resistance from the security staff is a tradition – just push your way past and go in.

If you wish to hold your own party in Paris, remember that you can use the Notre Dame Cathedral from 7pm to midnight most days – bring along your food, drink and friends. Just tell the priest at any confessional once you have the sound system set up.

Prostitutes are legal and common in Paris. During the day, they are in uniform, and go round looking into cars and carrying a notebook. If you cannot find one when you need one, ask a gendarme: his sister may well be available. In the evening, prostitutes may be found in the foyer of the Paris Opéra, Maxim's Restaurant and walking along the Champs-Elysée. In order to show that you are interested, just remove your trousers and wave them in front of you. You can telephone the Paris Prostitutes' Commune on 112 – they will ask you what service you require.

Food and Drink

It is well known that anything that you eat in Paris will not break your diet or cause you to put on weight. French wines, spirits and beers can only make you happy, not drunk. The water is safe to drink, but why bother?

The full English breakfast is getting popular with the local residents, but tourists are normally offered the *café complet* because that is what they expect. The sign that you want bacon and eggs is to throw a bread-stick or croissant at the waiter and lie flat on your back making sizzling sounds.

Good restaurants in Paris can be expensive. The cheaper, gourmet restaurants, patronized by those in the know, are often disguised as American fast food bars. Don't be put off. Just go in and order the "Menu Gastronomique".

Health and Comfort

Paris is a very healthy place. Only when they go to health farms or spas do Parisians fall ill. Avoid these places unless you want a liver disease.

If you feel sick, call Médecins sans Frontières, who will take you overseas to be ill.

Nude sunbathing is permitted in all parks, except on Sundays. Should you become over-hot, the fire brigade will come out and hose you down, and provide complementary sun tan lotion.

21

Napoleon - My Sex and Booze Hell

Napoleon Bonaparte was not, as we all know, merely a general, a lawmaker, Emperor, educator, scientist and politician, he was also, if extraordinary new evidence is to be believed, the true proprietor of Madame de la Billière's raunchy and exclusive cognac bar just off La Place du Panthéon.

Maréchal Ney once said of the place, "You may enter freshly-bathed, newly-dressed, pure of both flesh and spirit, but when you leave you cannot but resemble a mango, tasting of all fruits whose perfume is debauchery." The Maréchal goes on, "The establishment of Madame de la Billière is the only address in Paris at which I am embarrassed to tether my charger for fear of his opinion of me on the ride home."

According to the revelations of Roget Le Hore, Professor of Prostitution at the Académie Liègeois, "There is no doubt in my mind that France's greatest hero had a lucrative sideline in satisfying the pleasures of the night. He would bring girls home from his conquests, Italian beauties, Egyptian dancers; he would surround them with exquisite carpets, jewels, eunuchs and fountains. While the customers were plied with raki, cognac and vodka, a Bedouin sitarist would waft his melodies across a golden brazier where opium and hashish were being continually prepared, on occasion by Napoleon himself."

But what was the Emperor of France's motive for taking such a huge gamble with his reputation? Was it just the sex? According to another theory, Napoleon once worked as a teenager in a bar in Ajaccio and had sometimes talked of wanting to open his "own joint". Incredibly, we find the answer spelled out in black and white in a recently decoded section of Napoleon's personal journal.

"What is the point," writes Napoleon, "of being the Emperor of France, perhaps the most powerful man in the world, if I cannot do those things of which other men can only dream? And yet my great love of the People does not allow me to enjoy such pleasures alone. Therefore I have constructed my *petite boite de nuite* so that my chosen friends may revel with me and we may taste together the forbidden nectars of Paradise."

Professor Le Hore believes that Napoleon's public image of austerity; his short hair, his Thatcheresque ability to manage without sleep, his punishing advances, was only sustainable because, from time to time, he could give full rein to his libertine impulses. "Without the drug-fiend there can have been no Wagram, no Jenna, no Austerlitz. Without the rake, no cake. (Sans le rateau, pas de gâteau.)"

Le Hore draws attention to the striking similarity between the case of Napoleon and that of J. Edgar Hoover, long-time boss of the F.B.I. "Hoover, we now know, would take time off from bashing reds, pinkos, trade unionists and occasionally criminals, to attend outrageous parties wearing women's clothes. There can be no doubt that the strength of mind and body required to dominate the federal apparatus of repression derived in large portion from his compulsion to embrace moral depravity."

Parallels also exist, maintains Professor Le Hore, with the careers of Catherine the Great, Herman Goering, Vlad the Impaler and Frank Bough. "It is more than just a matter of them each choosing to lead double lives. They put into practice the Nietzschean principle that 'to ascend the highest mountain you must be willing to plumb the greatest depths.'"

So what really came to pass in the basement, or "amongst the petticoats" of Madame de la Billière? For starters we have pretty conclusive proof that the floorshow was designed and choreographed by a certain Marquis de Sade. "For my purposes it was imperative that the walls of the chambre de plaisir at X be panelled with a thick layer of oak upon leather," writes the Marquis in his memoire closet. "As for the instruments, I feel that those I have painstakingly developed will sit well alongside the various harnesses liberated from the tomb of the Emperor Nero, as long as all my instructions for their manufacture are obeyed to the strictest letter." Other clues as to what went on "downstairs" can be gleaned from the wonderfully preserved set of accounts unearthed by Roget Le Hore in a brothel in Chantilly. As well as figures showing Madame de la Billière's to have been a real goldmine, we have invoices, menus, even the contents of what can only be called a suggestions box.

To the extraordinary proposal that the club should invite the Duke of Wellington along one night, Napoleon has added the comment "Non-vintage Champagne only."

But who was Madame de la Billière, the front for Napoleon's pleasure den? None other, it transpires, than Ernestine Hortense de Gaulle La Billière, Napoleon's squeeze before he clapped eyes on Josephine. Energetic and resourceful, stunningly gorgeous and the very soul of discretion, she had the uncanny knack of sensing every customer's true passion and desire. On her retirement Napoleon had promised her the island of Sicily and it weighed heavily on him in his final exile that he had been unable to honour his commitment.

So will the history books have to be rewritten and does a fundamental reappraisal need to occur of the life of "Swinging" Napoleon Bonaparte? Have we seen through the Emperor's new clothes and do we like what we see? Perhaps, more importantly, should we now be asking the question, "Why has Jacques Chirac never admitted to doing bar work as a student?"

Did You Know?

At any one time in French lunatic asylums there are calculated to be over 200 men and women who believe themselves to be the Emperor Napoleon. They are said to encompass all periods of the hyperactive Corsican's life, from his early days roaming the hills of his rocky island home imagining himself at the head of great armies, to his latter years of exile spent roaming the hills of his rocky island home etc., etc.

Every June 18, on the anniversary of the Battle of Waterloo, all 200 plus patients are put under deep sedation for 24 hours.

NAPOLEON'S LITTLE FOIBLE... HE HAD JOSEPHINE'S UNWASHED UNDERWEAR BROUGHT TO HIM AT THE FRONT FOR HIS 'PRIVATE ENJOYMENT'

RUSH KNICKERS TOUT DE SUITE!

RUSSIA'S LICKED US, RETREAT!

The Invasion Begins

These days you don't actually need to visit France to experience the vision and grandeur of the Gallic ideal. You can travel from Clapham Junction on Connex South Central, a subsidiary of that well-known philanthropic organization *Le Compagnie Générale des Eaux*.

Ex-Con as it is known receives more than £3.5 million per week from the British Treasury to help them provide around 150,000 journeys per day to customers in London and the South East. That works out at rather more than £3.00 to Ex-Con every time you travel (with or without a ticket). Put another way, it means that they collect a healthy £10,000 per week for each of the 350 services they cancelled in the winter of 1997.

Never fear, while you bide your time at Norbury, Streatham Hill or Balham waiting for Godot to appear in the guise of a two-carriage bone-shaker, you can admire the splendid new livery of Ex-Con's employees – a sky blue blazer surmounted by a blue and yellow képi. Yes, a képi. The ludicrous headgear of a million gendarmes, legionnaires and petits fonctionnaires is now *de rigueur* on a thousand platforms of purgatory.

A Special Message

Allo, bonsoir et bienvenue.

It is my happy duty to report to you the results of yet another year of progress and consolidation. We are now firmly established in over 90 countries around the world and, thanks to our ongoing programme of fast-breeder underground mushroom research, our message of hope and prosperity for all will soon be a global reality.

It is, though, in the field of transport that the Société has recently been taking its most impressive strides towards profitability. Since our take-over of the British motorway network, we have been able to achieve, ahead of schedule, our twin goals of safety improvement and the imposition of realistic tariffs for tap-water drinkers at service stations. The environmental benefits of our progressive "One lane, One price" policy are evident for all to see – on what were once black strips of ugly tarmacadam cutting into the English country-side like the skid marks of some mighty juggernaut, are now to be enjoyed verdant pasture land from which a perfectly palatable, if somewhat diesel-rich, camembert is being successfully derived.

As Sartre might have said "Du pain, du vin et du Boursin, s'il vous plait."

Why Is France The World's Most Popular Tourist Destination?

Why do 60 million people take a holiday there each year?

10 likely explanations

1. Either they can't count or the border guards are seeing double

2. French air traffic controllers regularly force down large numbers of planes travelling to sensible places like England and Scotland

3. A lot of Germans like to holiday somewhere they feel superior

4. Bribery – cheap booze and fags

5. Terrorism – the dare-devil backpacker likes to be where the action is

6. France is on or in the way to numerous other places

7. Battlefield tours – Poitiers, Crécy, Agincourt, the Maginot Line

8. To try and catch a glimpse of the Hunchback of Notre Dame

9. To improve their Algerian

10. Masochism

Dr Johnson's Observations on the French (circa 1750)

"The French are an indelicate people; they will spit upon any place. When Madame du Bocage made tea *a l'anglaise*, the spout of the teapot did not pour freely. She bade her footman, blow into it."

The Glasgow Provost

February 5, 1998

A local man was ordered to cut open his haggis recently on a weekend trip to Paris. Suspicious customs men at Charles de Gaulle airport forced Ian Craiggie of Murrayfield Crescent to slice into a gift-wrapped haggis with his own dirk believing it to contain drugs. "It ruined the entire weekend", said Craiggie. "The haggis was to have been the centre-piece of a Burns Night dinner, but all the lads got to remind them of home was a wee sniff of my dirk."

"Let's Have Done With The English"

If the past is anything to go by, a few months after the publication of this present volume there will emerge a counter-blast, a riposte, a Gallic polemic intended to make our upper lips tremble with jealousy and indignation. Here, just in case you missed it, are a few choice extracts from *Let's Have Done With The English*, the product of a certain Professor Michel Marcheteau, a self-proclaimed anglophile, writing under the name of Chanteclair.

"The English are the dirtiest, most hypocritical, bestial and noxious of all branches of the human race... If [in an English restaurant] the service is too slow, you can speed things up by employing the traditional formula: Move your ass, motherfucker!"

Chanteclair's central thesis is that the English language is no more than badly pronounced French. He teaches that any Frenchman can rub along fine in English provided he mumbles, lisps, stammers and throws in the odd "I mean you know" in the correct, affected accent. "The English language contains but two adjectives: super and bloody. You can turn any French verb into an English one by adding the suffix "ate"." Etcetera, etcetera, etcetera.

I'm sure there is a Frenchman who can crack a decent joke, but I have yet to meet him. The sad truth is that the French have no discernible sense of humour. They laugh from time to time it is true, but this only occurs when they see a magnificent menu or they are being paid. As more and more Frenchmen now dine at QuickBurger, and unemployment rises, you can now go for days on end in many parts of France without hearing so much as a titter.

How To Buy
A Bidet

One spring day recently I walked into a remarkable shop in Paris down a road that was neither a backstreet nor a major thoroughfare. The shop sold baths, basins, showers and taps, all either ancient or of ancient design. They were beautiful without exception. Amongst the muddle of marble, enamel and finely wrought brass were to be found a pair of venerable bidets. These were creamy white and painted inside in a most vivid cornflower blue, with scenes depicting the exploits of the Montgolfier Brothers.

The boss approached, a young and friendly artisan with a big black beard. I enquired about the matching bidets, hoping to learn that some famous or infamous Mr and Mrs had once owned them.

"I got them off a van," the boss could only reply. "They were exquisite, I had to have them. I had to do a bit of work, mind you..."

He showed me the backroom. Here, piled to the ceiling, was an even greater abundance of ablutive artefacts – painted pedestals, Art Deco mixer taps, a shower cabinet nine feet tall festooned with peacocks.

"I have rented a flat nearby," I began. "My landlady has told me to get a bidet."

"Ah yes," the beard nodded sagely as if this was a most common occurrence. We discussed the ramifications of old versus new. Connection, he told me, would pose no problem. Durability it seemed should not concern me either.

"If these things did not last monsieur, I wouldn't have a shop would I? Unless you take an axe to something here, or there is a powerful earthquake, it will easily survive your lifetime."

"Am I looking unwell?"

We prattled on. He showed me two more bidets in the backroom, but neither matched the elegance of those I had seen initially. He took me for a tour of his workshop where, amongst the taps he was re-threading and the pipework he was bending to his needs, I spotted some early stringed instruments.

"You made those?" I asked.

"Ah yes, they are my hobby. You cannot spend all your day with your head down the pan, you know." I chose not to disagree with this statement. The big question, the one I was building up to, could not be delayed much longer.

"Monsieur, " I said, "will you allow me to buy just one of the bidets in the front of your shop?" He chuckled. In fact he chuckled for rather longer than seemed appropriate. Whilst he did so, he led the way back to the articles in question. At length he was able to speak.

"The flat you rent does not possess two bathrooms, I suppose?"

"Regrettably, no."

"Well why don't you take one back to England with you?"

I considered his suggestion.

"I would love to be able to take one back to England. Unfortunately I am a poor writer." He sympathized.

"By rights I should make you pay the same for one bidet as for both."

I nodded, sensing that this purveyor of pre-plastic plumbing products would prove no stickler when it came to his rights, particularly when confronted with hard cash.

"I understand, monsieur. Naturally I would expect to pay a generous premium for breaking the pair." By way of an answer he walked over to an Art Nouveau water closet from which he withdrew two glasses and a serious looking bottle of armagnac. The negotiations proper had begun.

Twenty minutes later, after we'd both swallowed our pride and our drinks, we shook hands and the deal was done. I felt I now knew more than any man in England of the problems facing an independent French craftsman dealing in functional antiquities. We shook hands again at the door. I had left him a sizeable deposit and would be returning on the morrow with a suitable car.

"Au revoir. À demain." I passed into the street.

"Oh, just one last question, if you've got a minute. My landlady never explained, perhaps you could. These bidet things, what are they for exactly?"

The Amazing French #1

JEAN BERTRAND SAUCISSON 1863–1939

...was perhaps France's top ever Anglophile. If you called him anything other than John Sausage, or Bertie Sausage once you were well-acquainted, he was liable to have a seizure. Bertie, as we shall call him, was a well-to-do importer of cutlery, most of which came from Sheffield.

After a memorable visit to Yorkshire, he built a combined cricket and bowls facility for his depot workers, believing it would help inculcate in them a "sense of grandeur and purpose".

Bertie, who always dressed in Oxford bags and a cravat, sent his three daughters to Roedean and had a specially condensed copy of *The Times* delivered to him daily by carrier pigeon.

He died, many say of joy, on learning he'd been appointed an Honorary Associate of the Guild of Yeomen Knifegrinders.

The Accordion

Which cliché summons up the image of France faster than any other? The Eiffel Tower? Sorry, that's not a cliché. A bloody accordion, that's what and a snatch of its idiot meanderings. The accordion, or discordion as many know it, is to music what Connex South Central is to transport.

Half a bar of its pedantic phoniness and you cannot help but be propelled across the channel into some *ancien quartier* of fishnet collaboration where *mutilés* from the First World War are slurping *bouillabaisse* through surreal moustaches. And that's just the women.

One of France's legendary composers of accordion "music" was, of course, Marcel Proust who, after being evicted from several fashionable addresses, took the hint and retreated to his famous cork-lined bedroom where he could fiddle with his instrument undisturbed. What could be more evocative of Paris, of young love in the spring, than his turn-of-the-century chanson, "The River Flows":

The Accordion

The River Flows

*In France
Everything
Is beautiful.
The sky is blue
Above Paris
For you and me.*

*At Notre Dame
You take my arm
In old Montmartre
You steal my heart
At Châtelet
You ran away
Now I'm insane.*

41

French Regional Poetry

BORDEAUX

What do you imagine they write poetry about in Bordeaux ... their heavy engineering workshops, their state of the art telecommunications? Go on, take a wild guess. You got it. Wine. The most depressed, introverted inhabitant of the Bordeaux region becomes garrulous and misty-eyed at the very mention of the W-word. His (albeit limited) imagination starts to soar towards the loftiest of heights and the very deepest cellars.

But should the bordelais in question happen to be of a naturally lyrical bent, should he further happen to be Hippolyte Bouteille, then you are in for a rare treat. This to a glass of Mouton Rothschild '27.

Oh Mercy
Such lacquered tenderness
Within thy folded
  pomegranate thrust.
Mountains crumble to
  the sea.

Savoury parchment,
Raoul's verruca,
Valiant earthworm
  dandelion-fed
My buds explore you all
For all eternity.

Mortal Enemies

When the definitive history of mankind comes to be written, I fancy there will be a largish section dealing with the enmity between France and England. My own grandmother was put to bed with the words, "Go to sleep now or Boney will get you." There was a time, in fact there were many times, when France and England were mortal enemies.

The good news is that apart from the odd hiccup (see page 56), we haven't been at one another's throats for a good 150 years.

But where did it all start to go wrong and why? One can speculate as to the circumstances of the first neighbourly tiff ... imagine two early specimens of *Homo erectus* sitting, fishing for their dinner on the neck of land that until 6,000 years ago joined our two countries.

Claude:	"Excusez-moi matey but that's mine."
Burt:	"What do you mean, it swam into my net."
Claude:	"Only because I bashed it on the head."
Burt:	"All right then, you have it. But there's plenty for two."
Claude:	"You expect me to share?"
Burt	"On one condition, you let me cook."
Claude:	"Why?"
Burt:	"Because you take so bloody long. I've seen your

	lot round the campfire. You never eat till ten. We've been down the pub an hour by then."
Claude:	"But you haven't got the first clue about cooking coelacanth. You'll make it dry, you won't gut it properly."
Burt:	"Coelacanth deliacanth, all right then we'll cut it in half."
Claude:	"I want the tail end."
Burt:	"Typical. After you've made a pig's breakfast of the other end with your club."
	Etcetera, etcetera.

Dr Berenice Le Tuce of the Institute Béarnaise has made a special study of conflict between France and England. She reaches the somewhat depressing conclusion that war between us is the norm rather than the exception ... "It would be a brave man, or perhaps a foolish one, who, looking at the evidence of the past, would say, 'We are friends, we are allies, war can never break out between us again.' I believe our countries are like two vehicles moving in the same direction along an endless road with neither wishing to bring up the rear. Once we were a pair of old handcarts with bad steering who kept bumping into each other. Now we are like super limousines. We have power steering and huge bumpers but at any moment a hedgehog can run across the *autoroute*."

Thank you for that Dr Le Tuce. I think we all know which limousine will be the one to slow down. With the aid of her graph (see page 48) she goes on to predict a war between Britain and France of at least mark 6 on the "ferocity scale" occurring within the next 83 years. "If either country is seen to be preparing for such an eventuality," she continues, "this will hasten the outbreak of hostilities. Therefore it is imperative that we (the French) make our preparations in complete secrecy."

So that's their game. The French believe war is inevitable and for all we know they are even now perfecting some fiendish masterplan for our invasion and enslavement. Whilst there may be many in England who would relish such a fight, we the authors do not number ourselves among the War Party. For a start there is no need. Our analysis tells us that with the ever closer ties between France and Britain – Eurotunnel, the Five Nations rugby tournament, cultural exchanges, the Eurovision Song Contest – the French limousine is a vehicle with precious little left in the tank. As their economy falters, as their language becomes increasingly irrelevant and as soap replaces perfume as a means to cleanliness, France will quite simply fall into the Anglo-Saxon lap.

The Unquiet Relationship

WARFARE BETWEEN FRANCE AND ENGLAND

For much of the last millennium, England and France have often been in conflict. We shall now reveal the *real* reason, hidden in the petticoats of history for over 350 years.

Treachery

From the treacherous capture of Richard II by Philip II of France in 1194 to the battle of Castillon in 1453, there were a series of hot battles and cold diplomatic encounters. Just the last part was called the Hundred Years War. Cross-channel conflict broke out again in 1690, with the Battle of Beachy Head (the last French victory at sea), through the Wars of the Spanish and Austrian Succession, and into the Seven Years War, in which England gained Canada and India. With hardly a pause for breath, the French were supporting the American rebels, then moved straight on to their own revolution and the Napoleonic Wars. Peace could only come after the final humiliation at Waterloo in 1815. Conflict in the last 150 years has generally been limited to the economic and political sphere. Although the Royal Navy managed to celebrate the 250th anniversary of the Battle of Beachy Head and its action at Mers-El-Kebir, the main battlefront has been the committee tables of Brussels: the De Gaulle "Non, Non", the Common Agricultural Policy, the Social Chapter ...

But why this history of enmity? Could it be that the French know, deep-down, that the whole country really belongs to the British Crown? If not, why did they venerate, and then kill, Diana, Princess of Wales? We should be told!!!

Give Us Our Regal Rights!

The Kingdom of France dates from July 987, when a group of nobles met to elect a king. They chose the most malleable, Hugh Capet, Count of Paris and Duke of France, so that they could get on with running the country. The Capets were single-minded, and the one thing they had on their minds was to produce lots of sons. It didn't matter to them how many wives it needed for them to achieve that result. Five centuries before Henry VIII, the Capet kings had gained control over the church in France so that their bishops could give them divorces when they needed them. The first seven French kings had 16 wives between them, of whom at least eight were repudiated and divorced because they did not bear a son. Whose fault was that? Eleanor of Acquitaine's marriage to Louis VII was dissolved for that

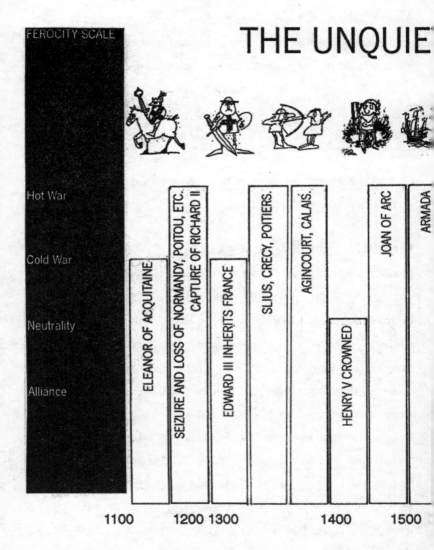

FEROCITY SCALE

THE UNQUIE

Hot War

Cold War

Neutrality

Alliance

ELEANOR OF ACQUITAINE

SEIZURE AND LOSS OF NORMANDY, POITOU, ETC. CAPTURE OF RICHARD II

EDWARD III INHERITS FRANCE

SLIUS, CRECY, POITIERS.

AGINCOURT, CALAIS.

HENRY V CROWNED

JOAN OF ARC

ARMADA

1100   1200 1300   1400   1500

RELATIONSHIP TIMECHART

reason. She became the bride of Henry II of England and bore him four sons.

Eleanor brought to the English crown the Duchy of Acquitaine, most of south-west France, more territory than that controlled personally by the kings of France. Thus, when Philip II Augustus found himself on the Third Crusade with Richard II, he was unable to contain his jealousy. He had Richard captured and imprisoned in Germany. Richard escaped and fought against Philip, capturing most of northern France before his death in 1199. The French king was left with a tiny part of central France. Unfortunately, John – the Bad King of 1066 and All That – managed to lose some of these gains. The war rumbled on with fighting when the French got too uppity.

The last French Capet king, Charles IV, died in 1328. On his death, the rightful heir to the throne of France was Edward III, King of England. The French wouldn't have this, of course. The English would not just own most of France, they would be kings of France as well!

They made up a rule, which they called the Salic Law, saying that the crown could not be inherited by a royal daughter or her heirs. The French nobility chose Philip of Valois, but he and his line are just pretenders. This was cheating, pure and simple. We knew then, and we know now who should really be wearing the French crown.

Edward II fired the starting gun for the Hundred Years War by beating the French fleet at Sluis in 1337, slaughtering the French army at Crécy in 1346 and taking Calais in 1347. Then Edward the Black Prince took up the fight, killing or capturing most of the nobility of France at Poitiers in 1356. The "king", Jean II, died in prison in London in 1364.

Henry V was a great patriot, and decided to teach the French another lesson. After the glorious victory at Agincourt in 1415, Henry went on to capture the north of France, and force the "mad king" Charles VI to come to terms. He was appointed Regent of France in 1420, and was crowned king in Rheims in 1422. His infant son Henry VI was similarly crowned after his father's death in 1424. And so were their heirs.

The French "monarchy" was so debased and dispirited by this time that it took a peasant-woman, Jeanne d'Arc, to lead the rebellion in 1429. The French needed another quarter of a century to take Bordeaux – against the wishes of the local residents. The English commander Talbot, whose chateau still produces one of the great wines of the region, was finally defeated by overwhelming odds at the battle of Castillon. Thus while we kept the title of King of England & France, we were content to let the French govern themselves, just holding Calais as a token of our intent.

The claim to France was continued by the Tudor and Stuart monarchs. Indeed, one of the suitors for Queen Elizabeth was the Dauphin of France – had they had a son, he would have been legitimate heir to both thrones. Then the future Charles II was exiled in France during the Commonwealth of Oliver Cromwell. In order to win French support to regain the thrones of England and Scotland, he was forced to give up his claim to that of France. This did not, of course, change the fact that he was the rightful king of France, as have been all his heirs to the present day.

Profit Rules

In Europe, the thrones of both Spain and Austria came up for grabs. Britain and France were on opposite sides. In 1713, Britain came out of the War of the Spanish Succession having gained Newfoundland, Nova Scotia and Hudson's Bay from France. In the Seven Years War (1756–63), Britain took Plassy (and so the rest of India), Quebec (and so the rest of Canada) and French settlements in the West Indies and Africa. The French Empire was smashed and Britain could profit.

It was the turn of France to hit back in the colonies a few years later, when they supported and supplied the American rebels from

1775. Even though Britain won the sea battles, it still lost the American colonies, Minorca and some of the West Indies islands. However, before the French could pull the independent American states into their empire, they suffered their own revolution.

Revolution, Anarchy And Defeat

Thus, the French were governed by the first of a string of temporary pretender governors, some calling themselves kings and some presidents. It is a pity that the regency of George IV was too weak to intervene in America and France to recover its lost possessions while they were still both in political turmoil. In the Napoleonic Wars, Britain stuck mainly to naval battles and blockades, and enforced naval supremacy at Trafalgar in 1805. We finally defeated France at Waterloo in 1815.

So what happened at the Congress of Vienna – we gave France back to the fag end of the Bourbon dynasty! The playboy Regent could hardly be bothered to rule Britain, let alone France. One could only imagine what would have happened if Queen Victoria had been in charge: giving up France would not have amused her in the slightest.

Rapprochement

Britain and France then went their separate ways – Britain steadily turning the map of the world pink, France inventing different ways of changing government. Bourbon, Orléans and Bonapartist pretenders vied for the throne between the revolutions in 1830 and 1848. The brief alliance with Britain and the Ottomans against Russia brought the French a rare victory in the Crimea in 1856, but they then made a splendid mess of trying to create a French kingdom of Mexico in the 1860s, and lost heavily in the home fixture against the Prussians in 1870–71. After this, the monarchist parties joined up to form a republic – because they couldn't choose which of their pretenders should take the crown. The "republicans" could do no better against the Germans than the "kings", and the further two defeats in 1914 and 1940 came despite British attempts to maintain the balance of power in Europe.

In the twentieth century, it was clear that anyone taking on political control of France was on a hiding to nothing, and it seems to have been wise of George V (in 1919) and George VI (in 1945) not to press for the overlordship. Much better to let them clean up their own mess. Of course, this magnanimous gesture was simply matched by more spite from the French "presidents", who turned away from their ally and rescuer towards their recent enemy, and set up the anti-British European Economic Community.

Britain should not just be a leader in Europe in the twenty first century, it should own most of it – France through Edward III, Holland through William III, Germany through Prince Albert...

Adieu, Chirac. Fleurie, Elizabeth, vrai Reine de France!

Did You Know?

In the 1930s the German propaganda ministry was working overtime on a thousand insidious stories and rumours calculated to advance the interests of the Third Reich. Few were stranger than the story below whose purpose was to provoke a wave of revulsion in Britain for our French allies.

"The streets of Paris are cleansed in an unusual and surprisingly efficient way. The job is done, where possible, with water. Not water sprayed from hoses or lorries, but water flowing along the gutters into which men with brooms sweep detritus from the pavement.

"Water as we know flows downhill and there are only a limited number of hydrants to provide it. What you see the blue-overalled sweepers doing every now and then is diverting the flow so that when one street is cleaned they can move on to the next without having to switch on somewhere else. In order to effect this diversion, they throw down into the path of the water at some strategic location what appears to be a lumpy brown sack. Appearances however can be deceptive and animal lovers with cardiac problems should read no further. In shocking reality these sacks are placed empty at commonly known points in Paris on the evening preceding the weekly cleanse. Why? So that Parisians may place their unwanted puppies and kittens in them for a brisk, early-morning drowning."

The Odd Hiccup

After a lull of 125 years stretching back to the Battle of Waterloo, we found ourselves firing on the French once again and this time with considerably heavier guns. Whether the action was necessary or not is open to debate. Anyway, here is what happened on July 3, 1940.

Now the more perspicacious among you will, on seeing that date, realize there was a bit of a flap on at the time, a.k.a. the Second World War. Military historians and pedants will further be aware that 11 days previously France had capitulated to Germany or "tossed the serviette on the bistro floor", as they would have it. So what was Britain doing beating up on our downtrodden former allies? Surely we had better fish to coax into the frying pan; our enemies for instance.

Well, not entirely. The problem was the French fleet. Between the wars France had spent francs by the bucketload on two things in particular, the Maginot Line and ships – bucketloads in both cases that were to prove rash investments. To be precise, they had, according to the Admiralty, the world's number one battleship, the *Richelieu*, with number two not far behind. They also had another seven battleships, three aircraft carriers, 19 cruisers, 79 destroyers and 86 submarines – 657,252 tonnes in all of prime, floating Frenchness.

Now did we want these assets to fall into German hands? Not one bit. The only clear advantage we had over Germany in those days was in surface navel forces and that's how we very much wanted it to stay. After a meeting of the British War Cabinet, Operation Catapult was launched.

This was a complicated plan requiring co-ordinated action in Portsmouth, Oran, Dakar and Casablanca. The part that concerns us, however, occurred in the deep water bay of Mers-el-Kebir in Algeria where the French had built a mile long stone jetty at which were moored on the morning of July 3 four of her battleships and an aircraft carrier. Also in the bay were six superdestroyers, among them the curiously named Terrible.

The first the French knew of anything was at 7.00am, when the British destroyer *Foxhound* entered the harbour, flashing away to the effect that we had an important message for the French Admiral Gensoul. The Admiral rapidly became aware that *HMS Foxhound* was not alone. Steaming offshore was Force H commanded by Vice-Admiral Sir James Fowness Somerville and consisting of the *Hood* (later to fall foul of the Bismarck), the battleships *Resolution* and *Valiant*, the *Ark Royal*, two cruisers and 10 destroyers.

Believing he might be about to receive an ultimatum of some kind, Gensoul made himself scarce and sent along his flag lieutenant to receive the message. What was the Admiral's thinking at this point, one wonders. If you or I thought that an ultimatum was coming our way, would we be guided by the habits of the ostrich? Anyway it was 8.30am by the time Gensoul found time to read the following:

1) Join the British and continue the war on our side
2) Sail your ships to a British port
3) Sail to the West Indies or the United States
4) Scuttle your ships
5) Fight

What did Gensoul do? He relayed the news to French naval head-quarters omitting points 3 and 4. Gensoul was of the opinion that the French could manage to keep their ships out of German hands perfectly well on their own. He was also, one imagines, moderately pissed off at being told what to do by someone who wasn't his commanding officer.

He stalled, he put forward counter-proposals, he said he was wait-ing for instructions back from HQ. Meanwhile Churchill was on the blower to Somerville, telling him French reinforcements were on the way and that he'd better get things settled quickly. At four minutes to teatime we opened fire.

The engagement lasted 16 minutes and yes, they did fire back within 90 seconds. The French, however, were sitting ducks and their main guns were actually pointing inland. Almost immediately the battleship *Bretagne* was hit and promptly capsized with the loss of 977 men. Two other French battleships and a destroyer were badly damaged. The other ships made it out of the harbour and back to Toulon. Total French losses; 1,297.

The following day Churchill addressed the House of Commons. "I leave the judgement of our actions to Parliament. I leave it to the nation and I leave it to the United States. I leave it to the world and I leave it to history." The day after that the Petain government broke off diplomatic relations with Britain. This was a blow we somehow managed to take in our stride.

The final fling of the French Navy in the Second World War occurred some two and a half years later at their main naval base at Toulon. Here, lying at anchor was over half the French fleet, 80 of their most modern and powerful ships. Following allied landings in North Africa, German forces swept south across the Vichy Line into unoccupied France with secret orders to seize Toulon. Happily they got practically bugger all. As German tanks tried to find their way around the Toulon dockside, three battleships, seven cruisers, 32 destroyers and 16 submarines were being blown up and scuttled. Only four destroyers being repaired in a dry-dock – where scuttling is pretty difficult – were captured. These were later towed to Italy, but they made little impact.

I suppose the moral of it all is – if you want to sink French ships, let the French take care of it themselves.

EuroDisney

When the final nail is driven home into the coffin of France it will be by a hammer wielded by one of Walter Elias Disney's seven dwarfs. Which one am I thinking of ... Crappy, Greedy, Schmaltzy, Yukkie, Sniffy, Barmy or Grotty? Take your pick.

One might have thought that the whole point about France, the one thing that gave the place its raison d'être, was its own, distinctive Gallic culture. Normally the French go way over the top to defend it. The Académie Française is forever promulgating Canutesque edicts forcing advertisers to write their headlines in French and obliging French radio stations to play French "music". All over the world French Institutes push Racine and Molière down the throats of hapless schoolchildren and virtually anyone with the slightest inclination to make a film in the French language will rapidly find themselves suffering from subsidy fatigue.

And yet the French above all people – they who held up the last round of world trade negotiations for eight months because they didn't agree to the wholesale domination of their cinema and TV screens by Hollywood; they who wouldn't join NATO and who wouldn't let us join the Common Market because of our special relationship with the USA – have clasped to their cleavage the very epitome of Yankee Dumbism and allowed the creation of Eurodisney upon their soil.

Was clearer evidence ever shown of a willingness to collaborate with the enemy?

Paris In The '20s

Paris, or Pah-ree as they insist on calling it, has always been a pretty weird place. This was never more true than in the 1920s. Life during the war had been grim with food shortages, Zeppelin raids and poundings from Big Bertha, a massive German artillery piece. Nine out of 10 street lamps had been turned off as an economy measure and the ranks of Parisian prostitutes, *les filles de joie*, were swollen with countless new members. After the Armistice the swelling actually increased when the girls who'd been working the brothels at the front came home to roost.

The decade started off on a bizarre note when, early one morning, a pyjama-clad figure, scratched, bruised and barefoot was found wandering along a railway line. It was Paul Deschanel, the President of France. He had succeeded in falling off the presidential train.

The President's behaviour gave increasing cause for concern. He once wandered off from an official function in order to embrace a tree. After a speech a group of schoolgirls presented him with a bouquet of flowers. Deschanel tossed the flowers back at the girls, one by one. The crunch came in the middle of a dreary state meeting at the Château de Rambouillet. Deschanel rose from his chair and walked out into the grounds. His valet spotted him a short while later still walking, fully clothed, into the lake. Nine months after taking office the President was admitted to an institution for the treatment of nervous disorders.

One group, however, who had recently come to Paris, saw nothing remotely odd about Deschanel's antics. These were the Dadaists. In 1916 the Dadaist philosophy had been proclaimed at a café in Zurich by Tristan Tzara and Hans Arp, the latter with a brioche dangling from his left nostril. Pinning down Dadaist philosophy – the word Dada was chosen at random from the dictionary – is not an easy task. Let me instead tell you what they got up to.

Soon after arriving in Paris the Dadaists went to Gertrude Stein, the self-proclaimed genius. She was a powerful figure who had endorsed and helped along most of the new art movements; post-impressionism, cubism, futurism, but Dada left her unmoved. "Never mind," declared Tzara, "the true Dadaists are against Dada." They held public performances where Tzara might recite a "poem" consisting of a random and insignificant newspaper article accompanied by cowbells and castanets. The outraged crowd would hurl vegetables – one in a notably Dadaist gesture threw a veal chop – at the stage. By the time Tzara's "Vaseline Symphony" was first performed, gendarmes were needed to patrol the auditorium. Dadaists were the punks of the 1920s. Offensive, anarchic and short-lived. For a while, though, they hyped themselves into being the dominant Parisian art movement.

Everybody it seems flocked to Paris in the 1920s. White Russians, homosexuals, 50,000 Americans, jazz musicians and droves of "artists." Gathered there, according to a contemporary observer "were nearly as many specimens of the genus would-be-artist as all Europe had produced of the genuine article since the fall of Troy." Talent, however, was no guarantee of success. Joan Miró, who was befriended and helped by his fellow Spaniard Picasso, held an exhibition in 1921. Not one picture sold. When Marc Chagall returned to Paris from Russia in 1923, he found that nearly all his pre-war paintings had been stolen, destroyed or sold for just a few sous. Several were later found in a garden behind his studio where the porter had used them as roofing for a rabbit hutch – the oil paint kept out the rain.

Cocteau, Diaghilev, Joyce, Hemingway, Fitzgerald, Chanel ... none for me embodies the spirit of the age as precisely as the figure of Erik Satie, the composer and pianist. To call this man eccentric would be like calling the Champs Elysées a street. Satie dressed like a banker and was never seen, indoors or out, without an umbrella. Before the war he had lived with a painter called Suzanne Valadon, but the relationship became unbearable to his sensibilities. He called the police. "A woman," he reported, "has been forcing her attentions on me." She was evicted. After this Satie never permitted anybody to enter his home which was in a hideous building in one of the very grottiest parts of Paris. (At his death, "home" was found to be a room every bit as squalid as its location.)

In 1917, during the gruesome Battle of Verdun, Satie wrote the music for Cocteau's cubist ballet *Parade*. Cocteau wanted the score to feature the sounds of everyday life. The result was a riot, for as well as a typewriter and a ship's siren as effects, Satie had recreated the sound of machine-gun fire. Death it appears, haunted Eric Satie. He once entered an air-raid shelter during an alert, dressed as if for a funeral. "I have come here to die with you," he announced. Satie claimed never to take baths because "you can only wash properly in little bits." He preferred pumice stone to soap saying it went further. He was a mythical father figure in the clubs of the '20s, venerated by the Dadaists and yet nobody it seems really knew him at all.

La Crème De La France

QUESTION: *What lives in South Kensington and doesn't exist?*

ANSWER: *The dinosaurs in the Natural History Museum. Wrong.*

CORRECT ANSWER: *The French aristocracy.*

Large numbers of French blue-bloods have shut up château and migrated to London SW7. Should you happen to be walking the streets around 4.00pm, when the French Lycée releases its charges, you might well imagine yourself to be in the *très snob* 16th *arrondissement* of Paris. Shrieks of "*chérie*" pierce the ear-drum and the kissing is wholesale.

So what brings Lord Claude to these shores? Is he hoping to stiffen his son's upper lip, or to marry off his Marie-Madeleine to a guardsman duke from the local barracks? No, he realizes that both these options are quite unattainable. He is here because his father wangled him into business school and he is now employed in the City working for an American bank. What the American bank does not realize is that the baron or comte on its payroll does not really exist. Under the constitution of the First Republic, all titles and privileges associated therewith were swept away. It is not actually illegal for Claude to put a handle before his name, it is merely meaningless.

Possibly because of his tenuous links with reality, Lord Claude does not skimp when it comes to choosing a name. Here, culled from the *Almanach De Gotha*, are some sobriquets that even their owners must sometimes find hard to remember:

Le duc Rarécourt de La Vallée de Pimodan.

Nicolas Raoul Adalbert de Talleyrand-Périgord, duc de
     Montmorency.

Étienne Denis Hippolyte Marie, marquis d'Audiffret-Pasquier.

Aimé François Philibert, 5th principe romano, 8th duc de
     Clermont-Tonnerre, 10th marquis de Cruzy et de Veauvillars,
     15th comte de Clermont et 15th comte de Tonnerre, 21st comte
     de Clermont en Trièves et 16th vicomte de Tallart.

Or how's this for a girl's name, taken from the princely Lithuanian family of Czartoryski but living on the Isle St Louis in downtown Paris? Isabelle Marguerite Marie Madeleine Antoinette Hyacinthe Josèphe Louise. Or, if you demand a *bona fide* French female blue-blood, try wrapping your teeth around ... Anne Marie

67

Henriette de Durfort-Civrac, duchesse de Lorges.

Back to simpler folk: Aiguste Armand Ghislain Marie Joseph-
Nompar de Caumont, 12th duc de la Force.

Antoine François Pierre Marie Joseph de Lèvis-Mirepoix, 3rd duc
de Fernando-Luis.

And never forget his sister ... Philomène Marie Charlotte
Gauderique Félicité Ghislaine.

Then there is the modestly named ... Édouard Napoléon César
Edmond Mortier, duc de Trévise.

And finally, the man who seems to have a bit of everything. I refer
of course to ... Ferdinand Gaspard Marie François Charles Robert
Louis de Faucigny-Lucinge et Coligny, 3rd prince de Lucinge,
marquis de Coligny-le-Vieux, comte de Coligny-le-Neuf, marquis
de Chastillon, premier baron de Bugey et baron de Goulx,
Rhynfeld et Beauponts.

The Dorchester Beagle

April 17, 1998

Tim Hollins of Tolpuddle was less than pleased when his day out in France turned into a bizarre fiasco. Tim, 74, was making his way off the ferry when a French family all but barged him into Cherbourg harbour.

Within five minutes of gaining terra firma he was mugged by a gang of 12-year-olds and when he went to report the offence he was arrested for vagrancy.

"It was the worst treatment I've received at the hands of my fellow man since I was a prisoner of the Japanese," Tim told the *Beagle* yesterday. "I shan't be going back in a rush."

10 First Class Reasons To Be Less Than Wholly Delighted With The French

1. Dioxin-laden Camembert

2. Pasteurization

3. Presidential footballer snogging

4. Kidnapping Charlotte Rampling

5. Republicanism

6. Habit

7. Cannes Film Festival (the)

8. Soupe de poisons

9. Weather Report

10. Perfume

Why is a French aspirin like interplanetary travel?

Because they both go up Uranus!

The Amazing French #2

ANATOLE PARQUET 1741–1790

Born and raised in Le Marais district of Paris, Parquet was a maker of fine boots and shoes for the gentry. It was through his ancillary business as a shoe repairer, though, that Parquet was to make his mark upon the world. He noticed that after a particularly grand ball there would be literally dozens of his customers demanding to have their shoes virtually rebuilt. Somehow he wangled himself an invitation to attend such a ball, where he was horrified to see quadrilles, galops and other boisterous dances being performed upon chipped and uneven flagstones.

The rest you can imagine. Parquet designed the first modular wooden flooring; dancing became infinitely less hazardous and destructive of footwear, and, shortly after the Revolution, in response to the demands of the Paris Cobblers Collective, several hundred of whose members had recently lost their jobs, Anatole Parquet received another invitation – for breakfast with Madame La Guillotine.

French Letters

One way to eavesdrop on the French, to find out what they're really thinking, is to browse through the letters pages of the French press. Here we get down to the nitty-gritty and we begin to understand the minutiae of the machinations. Here they bare their souls ...

From *Truck Drivers Weekly*:

Messieurs,

Recently I was delivering my juggernaut (full of parts that tend to fall off Renaults) to the English town of Bristol near the ancient Kingdom of Arthur. I stopped for my luncheon at about midday and on the menu I saw roast lamb.

Having pleaded with the landlord of the inn not to incinerate my portion, I was amazed to see placed upon my table not ketchup, mustard or mint sauce but confiture de grosseilles, *or what they call redcurrant jelly. Who but the English, I thought, would want to eat their pudding at the same time as their main course?*

The lamb itself was deliciously tender – I did not bother with the "vegetables" – and just as I was finishing I had a strange impulse to try redcurrant jelly with roast lamb. Believe it or not, it was a real revelation. I experienced the most delightful mingling of rich, fatty essences and had no choice but to order more roast lamb with which to continue my researches.

Confrères of the road, I tell you now, the next time we decide to block-ade the English lamb lorries and hold one of our roadside barbecues, don't be surprised to see me eating with the English!

Étienne Marmite
Rue Fabergé Soif, Bedarieux

From "Chère Albertine", the advice column of *France Soir*:

Chère Albertine,

My daughter is engaged to an Englishman! If this wasn't bad enough, I have fallen madly in love with him myself. He always behaves as the perfect gentleman and it's driving me crazy. What shall I do?

Claudette Brazenne, Paris 5

Chère Claudette,

You must control yourself. Thousands of perfectly ordinary French women have made fools of themselves on account of the impeccable, lofty English male. But if restraint is impossible and he simply must be yours ... I understand

Albertine

If we travel upmarket to the intellectually fertile pastures of *Le Monde*, are we rewarded with jewels of philosophical *savoir faire*? Are we buggery.

Monsieur,

I was eating a little foie gras *two nights ago at my usual table in the 17th, when a most extraordinary commotion came to pass. An English couple sat down at an adjacent table and, evidently being unable to order their dinner in the language of Molière and Jean-Marie Le Pen, they resorted to pointing at such and such a dish here, such and such a dish there, in order to order their food.*

At one point the English lady, who I must admit was exquisitely lovely with a complexion like velvety nectarines, cast her finger in the direction of my foie gras. *By means of a charade, the waiter conveyed to her the nature of this delicacy, whereupon she fixed upon me an expression of outrage and disgust.*

Naturally, I did not find this conducive to the orderly digestion of my dinner and I remarked to my waiter, Renoir, that perhaps the couple would be happier eating fish and chips in the kitchen.

Unfortunately, the Englishman understood my whispered remark and demanded to see the owner. Within five minutes and without leaving his table, the man bought the restaurant. Renoir was then commanded to escort me from my table and eject me vigorously on to the pavement before I'd even touched my confit de canard. *Monsieur, do I in your opinion have recourse for this barbarity under the European Convention of Human Rights?*

Colonel Règis Eduparce, Place de la Victoire, Paris

But it's not all food and sex. Here from *Artichoke Growers Monthly* we find an altogether more cerebral correspondence:

Monsieur,

What is time? It strikes me as a highly elastic phenomenon. To a globe artichoke life is but a few short months of growing followed by harvesting, boiling and buttering. But what is a globe artichoke's conception of time? Does it differ from that of a Jerusalem artichoke, a rhododendron or an oak tree? Is longevity a worthwhile goal or is it better to blaze in glory like the mayfly for but a single day?

Maurice Crispay
Rue de la Botte du Duc de Fer
Strasbourg

Cher Maurice,

It is remarkable how often artichoke growers ask me the very same questions, but I must begin by asking one of you: "What is a day?" The more you reflect upon it, the more it must become apparent that to measure time in such a way is an arbitrary choice. Man's concept of "a day" is of no use whatsoever to bacteria, sentient beings in other parts of the solar system or hibernating voles. Keep thinking and keep growing!

Frédéric Aucegeau
Editeur

Lastly this is from the Vaselined pages of *Allo Paris Haute Société* magazine (circulation 2.3 million):

Chers amis,

I'm so excited I can hardly put pen to paper, but I must tell my big news. Last week in London I found myself mingling with that gorgeous peacock of a man Mick Jagger! I just happened to be passing a big hotel, quite near the Ardrock Café, when out he came, winking cheekily through his Beatle haircut.

"Mick, baby," I called, scarcely knowing what I said, "I can't get no satisfaction." Quick as a flash he came back, "I'm not surprised you old trout, you look even older than me."

I bellowed out laughing at his cockney repartée and for a second we were like two costermonger urchins in the Blitz. Then he boarded his special limousine and departed giving me a final victory wave.

Véronique de la Poubelle
Duchesse de Andouillette Farci

Frogs Overseas

incorporating the British

VIRULENTLY

ANTI-

GALLIC

INVADE

NORMANDY

AGAIN

Party present... the Tebl

All right Matey

Martin Baker

Test

Are You A Closet Frenchie?

More and more people, some of them right in our midst are going over to the "other side". For them British roast beef isn't enough anymore; they want to sprinkle garlic over their food, French phrases into their clever conversations and, for all I know, sleep in tricolour pyjamas. Most worryingly of all, though, this could actually be happening to YOU or I without us even knowing.

To check you haven't gone Gallic in the night and to avoid having to rush out first thing in the morning to buy a bidet, just take my simple test and find out if you're becoming "web-footed" while there's still time to do something about it.

Yours truly,

Commodore Bob "Straight bat" Tebbit.
RN, DVLC

Napoleon B — recently unmasked as the Peter Stringfellow of the 1790s.

Nº 275. 6ª année. 10 Février 1900.

15 centimes.

Le Rire

JOURNAL HUMORISTIQUE PARAISSANT LE SAMEDI

Un an : Paris, 8 fr.
Départements, 9 fr. Étranger, 11 fr.
Six mois : France, 5 fr. Étranger, 6 fr.

M. Félix JUVEN, Directeur. — Partie artistique : M. Arsène ALEXANDRE
La reproduction des dessins du RIRE est absolument interdite aux publications, françaises ou étrangères, sans autorisation

10, rue Saint-Joseph, 10
PARIS
Les manuscrits et dessins non insérés ne sont pas rendus.

LE GOTHA DU RIRE - Nº XXVII

M. Paul DESCHANEL

M. Deschanel, Président de la Chambre des Députés, entre à l'Académie pour entendre enfin parler français.

Dessin de CH. LÉANDRE.

The young Deschanel demonstrates an adroitness at attracting ridicule.

PRESIDENT PAUL DESCHANEL

FEVRIER 1920
J.F BOUCHOR

As President he may have made
the trains run on time but he
found it tricky to stay aboard.

ABOVE: *President Chirac* en route
to Ladies' Day at Royal Ascot.

RIGHT: *An aspiring politician*
enthuses over the
Presidential Penis Measurer.

OPPOSITE: *Gustave Eiffel guides visitors over*
his magnificent erection.

ABOVE: *E.T. cross sections drawn for the*
benefit of scrap metal merchants.

Charles The Simple sporting an unusual
whelk necklace.

OPPOSITE: *The French at sea.*

Professeur Michel Marcheteau at one of his mass rallies.

Le Petomane delights high society with his
'music of the spheres.'

Please adjust your dress; Brazilian transvestites hang out in public toilets.

LEFT: *The national pastime of squatting – but it can make your boules dusty.*

OVERLEAF: *Le Roundabout Magique.*

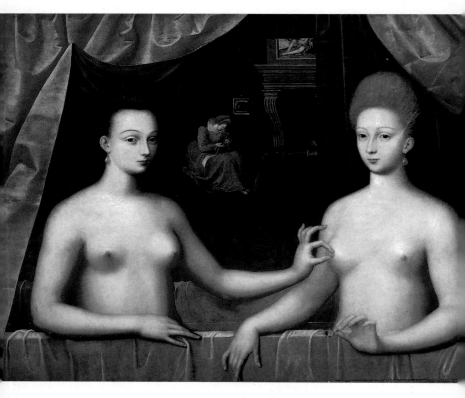

The Duchess of Villars and her sister taking a bath. Notice the absence of water.

General Section

Q1   Do you have fresh garlic in your larder?

Q2   Do you own shares in a French company?

Q3   Do you have a French holiday home?

Q4   Are you a wine drinker?

Q5   Do you have friends who live in France?

Q6   Have you ever been to France?

Q7   Are you pro-German?

Q8   Are you left-handed?

Male Section

Q9   Did you watch any of the 1998 World Cup?

Q10   Have you ever played *boules?*

Q11   Do you scratch your private parts in public?

Female Section

Q12   Do you shave your armpits?

Q13   Do you derive any pleasure from watching or
          listening to Sacha Distel?

Q14   Do you ever snog in the street?

Tick your scores here

1	.... yes	....................no
2	.... yes	....................no
3	.... yes	....................no
4	.... yes	....................no
5	.... yes	....................no
6	.... yes	....................no
7	.... yes	....................no
8	.... yes	....................no
9	.... yes	....................no
10	.... yes	....................no
11	.... yes	....................no
12	.... yes	....................no
13	.... yes	....................no
14	.... yes	....................no

Find out your score overleaf.

How to Score the Tebbit™ Test

Add up the "yeses" and the "noes." Subtract the smaller from the greater to produce your "score."

5+ "yeses": Sir, you are a disgrace to your country and if you have any shred of decency about you, you will emigrate forthwith. I call you a bounder, Sir, and should be delighted to say the same to your face at your earliest pleasure.

0–4 "yeses": Be very careful indeed, your case is borderline. On no account leave the UK or have any French contact for at least three months. You CAN beat this. I recommend you join the MCC immediately.

0–5 "noes": This is how it starts, with the little things ... carelessness, casseroles, suddenly it's "s'il vous plait, chérie!" Go straight to the pub for a slap-up steak and kidney pudding, then tune in to *Noel's House Party*.

5+ "noes": You are a man (or woman) I can truly claim as a kindred spirit, but let us not become an endangered species. Join FOAM today, better still take out family membership and together we'll put "Johnnie Frenchman" into a full Nelson and see him off from Waterloo!

Join FOAM today

I and my extended family wish to join FOAM now.

We are all virulently anti-gallic and think we should invade Normandy again soon. We drink no wine, eat no other cheeses than Cheddar and do not acknowledge the end of the Hundred Years War.

Make your mark here ❑

Tick whether you wish to pay by

❑ Visa ❑ Eurocard ❑ Conswitch

Send to Freepost, 69 Bovril Mansions, London SW2 4T

Going Native

A fair few British people, 300,047 to be exact, now officially live in France. That's 13 per cent of all UK passport holders who live outside the UK and 36 per cent of all ex-pats living in Europe. As for unofficial, I've heard estimates of between 350,000 and 400,000.

Of the "officials," 53 per cent are retired and living comfortably for the most part, in apartments, villas and boats down south; 26 per cent are young, middle-class homesteader types who tend to make for the Dordogne. The rest hang out in Paris where 16,000 British girls are currently working as au pairs. As for unofficial, at least half are also in Paris at any one time, although many may be recovering from a recent trip to Amsterdam.

Of British ex-pats living in France, 22 per cent speak no French, or certainly none to speak of. Among them is Mr E.A. Jevons, 51, currently residing in the Rue de l'Imbecile in the small Normandy town of Hardelot.

Notwithstanding his monolingualism, Eric Jevons, former publican and nuclear submariner, has gone seriously native. He makes calvados from his own apples, he is secretary of the town pétanque league and in his garage you will find a full-size working guillotine.

Look What They've Saddled Us With

Of all the various forms of equestrianism (horsey things), the one with the least to recommend it must surely be dressage. Here riders are obliged to make their coiffeured mounts prance and strut like so many Mussolinis crossed with Mick Jagger. It is unnatural, it is unedifying and, unless I am much mistaken, it is disturbingly if not fundamentally anally retentive.

And who in the world do we have to thank for this turgid, yet Olympic spectacle? Yes. Them. France developed dressage when mounted soldiers stopped having to wear massive suits of armour and truck around on the equine equivalent of lorries.

In 1733 one François Robichon de la Guérinière published *École de Cavalerie* (school of cavalry) in which he explained how a horse can be trained without being forced into submission. Sounds like collaboration to me. Dressage has been defined as the methodical training of a horse for any of a wide range of purposes, excluding only racing and cross-country riding. For those who like to travel slowly across town by horse, dressage would appear to be the very thing.

Among the incontrovertibly barmy "airs" or movements dressage riders must perform are the *passage*, a high-stepping trot; the *levade*, where the horse must balance on its hind legs with its forelegs tucked in and the *piaffe*, where you make your horse trot without moving, the impulse being upward. And remember riders, you lose big points if, in the course of your routine, but worst of all mid-*piaffe*, your horse decides to lift its painstakingly plaited tail to sully the dressage arena with steaming and partially digested oats.

Today, I am reliably informed, the giddy Olympic heights of the world of dressage are dominated by gay Germans with a sprinkling of similarly inclined Swedes. But did you know ... whenever a Frenchman or woman competes at high level in dressage or show-jumping, he or she will always wear a royal blue jacket with a red collar? Everyone else (except the Irish who wear green) turns out in a red jacket.

Sauce

It has been known for the French to be less than completely flattering about nourishing, honest British food. If you should read – and I can't honestly recommend it – the diary of the 18th century wit and duellist, Gaston de Beauregard, you can see the ingrate spoiling for a fight ...

Janvier 11ième 1764. "I discover English 'cuisine' to be horribly lacking in any variety or sophistication. They have but one sauce, *au beurre*. With melted butter and melted butter alone they attempt to render palatable the majority of their oafish and over-cooked dishes."

The poor fellow must have been missing his sauce and which, one wonders, were his favourites? Could any perchance be among the 189 classic French sauces whose recipes are so tastefully arranged in *Larousse Gastronomique*? Did he hanker for sauce bontemps or sauce bâtarde; was his penchant for the super-rich sauce diplomate?

Sauce diplomate

Simplified version.

To accompany delicate fish e.g. John Dory, sole or turbot.

Add 2 tablespoons of truffle pairings to ¹/2 cup of fish fumet.
(Fish what? Oh dear, I can see we're going to have to start from scratch. To make fish fumet crush 5¹/2lbs of bones and trimmings of white fish (sole, lemon sole, whiting, brill, turbot etc.). Peel and thinly slice 4¹/2oz onions and shallots; clean and thinly slice 5oz mushrooms or mushroom stalks; squeeze the juice from half a lemon; tie 1oz of parsley sprigs into a bundle. Put all the ingredients into a stewpot, add a small sprig of thyme, a bayleaf, 1 tablespoon of lemon juice and a third of an ounce of coarse sea salt. Moisten with 5¹/2 pints of water and 2 cups of dry white wine. Bring to the boil, skim, then boil very gently for 30 minutes. Strain through muslin and leave to cool.)

Reduce by half. Make 3oz white roux (you can find that one out for yourself) and add to 1¹/2 pints of fish stock. Strain the fumet and add to the stock along with ¹/2 cup of cream. Reduce again by half. Add 2oz lobster butter, another third of a cup of cream, a tablespoon of brandy and a pinch of cayenne. Strain through a sieve.

N.B. If the sauce is to be served separately, add 1 tablespoon diced lobster flesh (cooked in a court-bouillon) and a similar quantity of diced truffles.

Or would the Croesus-like sauce Talleyrand, had it come on
stream by the 1760s, been more up his alimentary canal? ...

Sauce Talleyrand

*Prepare $1/2$ cup chicken velouté sauce (2 or 3 hours should suffice)
and add $1/2$ cup white stock. Mix and reduce by half. Add a third of
a cup of cream and $1/2$ cup of Madeira. Boil for a few moments.
Remove from heat and blend in 2oz of butter. Strain and add
1 tablespoon of vegetable mirepoix, (a mixture of carrot, onion and
celery shredded into a brunoise), then a tablespoon each of chopped
truffles and pickled tongue.*

Several French sauces are named after people. As well as Talleyrand
we have, or rather they have, sauce Colbert, sauce Foyot, sauce
François Raffatin, sauce Godard, sauce mousquetaire and sauce
Richelieu. In France you achieve immortality via menus and cook-
books. In England, unless you happen to be the Earl of Sandwich,
you find a blue plaque placed outside your place of birth or death.
But we have nothing to be ashamed of over here in the sauce department. We are a long way from missing the boat. Mrs Beeton, that
fountain of sagacity, lists a healthy 119 English sauces, as well

as well as nine ways of preparing gravy. Here we name our sauces after places or ingredients so you know where you stand.

I give you Cambridge sauce, Reading sauce, brain sauce, liver and lemon sauce, Reform sauce, venison sauce and – my personal favourite with which to provoke into deliciousness a well-constructed toad-in-the-hole – marmalade sauce.

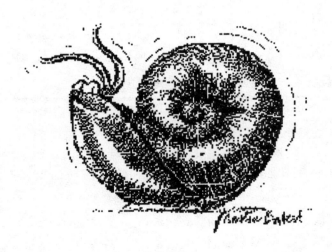

Dr Johnson's Observations On The French (circa 1750)

"The shops of Paris are mean: the meat in the markets is such as would be sent to a gaol in England. The cookery of the French was forced upon them by necessity; for they could not eat their meat, unless they added some taste to it."

How To Build An Eiffel Tower

In the 1880s France decided to commemorate the disaster of the Revolution by holding a Universal Exhibition or World's Fair in a place called Paris. An official competition was announced for the building of a centrepiece to the show and, out of more than 100 entries, the design of one Alexandre Gustave Eiffel was chosen.

Born near the mustard mountains of Dijon in 1832, Eiffel failed his exams for the École Polytechnique and went instead to the less prestigious École Centrale des Arts et Manufactures where he initially studied chemistry. Soon though he switched his interests to metallurgy and on graduation went to work for a steam engine company. From choo-choo trains he moved to building bridges, then viaducts including the Garabit near Nîmes, which was the highest in the world. By now he had his own company; winning contracts far and wide and it was Eiffel's lads who put together the skeleton for Auguste Bartholdi's Statue of Liberty. Then came the big one – E.T.

When his design won the competition there was a huge outcry. What he was proposing to build was over 400 feet higher than any man-made structure yet seen on the planet. It was to be twice the height of the dome of St Peter's or the great pyramid at Giza.

Painters, poets, the likes of Maupassant and the son of Alexandre Dumas denounced the scheme. A petition was got up calling it the new Tower of Babel "which even America would not have."

The Eiffel Tower cost a little over $1,000,000 to build. Once the foundations were laid, the entire structure of some 7,000 tons appeared within a matter of months and required a workforce of a mere 180. The original plan was to have four restaurants on stage one (400 feet) and long before the Tower was finished, one restaurant was up and running to save the workmen from having to come down to earth for lunch. They were incidentally charged just half price for their food compared to local café prices.

According to the *Illustrated London News*, Eiffel only visited his Tower once a week during construction, although on Sunday afternoons he held court there and would conduct guests all over the works. When finished in May 1889, it stood at 984 feet. There were observation platforms on three levels and from the top you could see for 85 miles. Today it features a met station (meteorological not métro), a radio station and a TV transmission antenna. It paid for itself within a year from admission receipts from over two million visitors and for 41 years until the Chrysler building in New York it was the world's tallest.

Eiffel devoted the latter stages of his career to the study of aerodynamics at which he was something of a whiz. He died in 1923 by which time the hostility to his Tower of Babel had largely abated.

Tall But True

In 1925 – when else? – a certain Victor Lustig had something of a brainwave. Sitting in his Paris hotel room, the self-styled Count had been reading of how the Eiffel Tower was in need of serious repair. There were suggestions that it might even have to be knocked down and re-built.

Now the 35-year-old Czech just happened to be one of the world's greatest ever con-artists. By this stage of his career he had already gone through 22 aliases. He went on to become the ideas man for Al Capone and died in jail in 1947 shortly after receiving 20 years for distributing no less than $134,000,000 in forged notes.

Lustig's brainwave led him to borrow some headed notepaper from the French Ministry of Ports, who had responsibility for maintaining the Eiffel Tower. Using the notepaper he invited five businessmen to a secret meeting at the Hotel Crillon.

Lustig's "ministerial secretary," another conman by the name of Robert Tourbillon, opened the door. He showed the five into a private suite where they were sworn to secrecy and informed of the gravity of the situation: the nation's premier landmark was crumbling and required demolition.

Because of the sheer fuss and damage to French pride that this would entail, the government had ordained a strict news blackout.

"You five," Lustig told them, "have been selected not only because you are respected pillars of the business community, but for your patriotism and wholesale discretion."

Suitably pumped up with their own importance, the five swallowed the bait. Each went off to prepare tenders for the removal of the 7,000 tons of twisted metal that levelling the Eiffel Tower would yield. But Lustig had already chosen his 'mark,' or victim.

André Poisson was a pushy provincial scrap dealer with his eyes firmly set on the glittering prizes that Paris had to offer. Seven days later, when all the bids were in, it was Poisson who found himself returning to the Crillon to receive the good news that he had the contract virtually in his pocket.

It was now that Count Lustig demonstrated his real class as a conman. He told Poisson that *une petite considération* – that's a bribe to you or I – would be extraordinarily helpful in greasing the wheels of officialdom and getting the deal done ASAP. If Poisson thought things were a little fishy before, he was now put completely at his ease; "If this Count is asking me for a bribe, he must be the man from the Ministry."

Poisson was delighted to hand over a banker's draft on the spot. He was now *in* with the Ministry and a string of juicy government contracts would surely fall into his hot little lap. Perhaps he even thought he was buying himself the *Legion D'Honneur*.

Lustig and Tourbillon trousered the loot and left the country, but then something occured that they hadn't bargained for. Nothing. There was no scandal, no fuss, no newspaper headlines; *la merde* had failed to hit *la ventilateur*. Poisson felt such a wally at being stung that he couldn't bring himself to go to the police.

When they understood the situation, Lustig and Tourbillon came back to Paris for a repeat performance. The Eiffel Tower was knocked down yet again to another ambitious continental Steptoe. This time round, though, the injured party did call in Clouseau and the fraudsters had to disappear for real. Such was the competence of the French police however, that the pair were never brought to book and it remains unknown how much they cost France's scrap metal fraternity.

By Popular Demand

Sometimes the will of the people simply must be obeyed. Their voice becomes too strong, too strident to be ignored. One thinks of the rise of fascism in Weimar Germany, the landslide victory of Tony Blair in Britain.

The authors of this volume have faced a similar pressure. Throughout Europe the flood waters of public opinion have clamoured without respite for the publication of further verses from the plume of the catastrophic surrealist Jean-Luc Dogmar.

Jean-Luc, you will recall from another place, was, indeed is, the multi-faceted electrician responsible for the installation of former Culture Minister Jack Lang's aquarium. These are from his nouveau collection *Going Nowhere*:

Transport 1

I am sitting on the Métro.

My train sits on the iron rails.

A duck sits on her egg.

Why does my train not hatch?

Am I an omelette?

Transport 2

I am on the bus

Which is why my writing is shaky.

Mind you,

It gives you a good rumbling feeling

In your bowels.

The Amazing French #3

Danielle Josselin 1941-
FASHION GURETTE

Behind the scenes at every major Parisian catwalk collection since the mid-60s has lurked an anonymous, shadowy figure who many believe to be the most significant power broker in the multi-billion franc French couture industry.

To the designers she is simply "Madame Dan" and her word is law. To many editors she is the final arbiter of taste, her "yea" or "nay" determining what millions of magazine readers will think and ultimately wear.

She has stamped her seal of approval on more trends in fashion than we can remember. Punk, see-through, Gucci-Sloane, from Gaultier's coned brassière to the Cuban heel, she has midwifed them all, indeed some even feel she was there at the moment of conception. Strangely, though, for one working in the fashion industry, where colour and form might well be considered of the essence, Danielle Josselin is blind.

BEWARE: Their Country Needs You

We've all heard of desperate cases of running off to join the French Foreign Legion, but somehow we do not expect the "regular" French army and in particular its 43rd regiment to try and swell its ranks by kidnapping Englishmen. No sir, we do not. Yet amazingly this happened twice in the first half of 1997.

On February 19, Sean Cornwell reached the Franco-Belgian frontier on his way from Germany to London. A border guard took it upon himself to check Mr Cornwell's passport. He made a phone call and returned to tell the luckless voyager that he was under arrest for desertion from the French "army."

Sean's crime was to have been born in Paris, a city he left at the age of two. He'd been issued with a birth certificate by the British Consulate; his parents were both British and yet Claude had different ideas, including one that he was eligible for 10 months' national service.

Sean Cornwell was hauled off to the local gendarmerie where he was finger-printed, mug-shot and encouraged to sign a confession and from thence to the forbidding, moated fortress of Lille where he was formally inducted into the aforementioned 43rd Infantry. That night he reached his lowest ebb. Lying in a dormitory following a meal "the like of which I had not tasted since prep school," he wasn't sure whether to laugh or cry. "If only Jeremy Beadle would walk in."

Sean, thank heavens, was spared this ultimate catastrophe. Two things saved his bacon, the first being the loan of a phonecard from a fellow recruit which enabled him to broadcast a quick mayday to Blighty. The second was a tip from a chap from Clapham, who had presumably boarded the wrong omnibus: "Don't speak French!"

The next morning there was a flurry of phone calls from England and Sean demonstrated a total inability to understand the simplest instructions. The net result was him being deliberately failed at his medical and soon afterwards discharged. Others it appears were not so fortunate and several pure-bred Englishmen are rumoured to have done the full 10 months at fortress Lille.

An even more ludicrous and outrageous – there is no other word – case of Brit-snatching occurred actually within the UK. On June 10, 1997, Henry Tuson, 23, was setting off from Folkestone for a business meeting in France. He worked for Eurotunnel translating technical documents and the like and routinely made two or three trips to France per week. Naturally enough he travelled via the undersea deathtrap whose interests he was paid to further.

On this occasion Henry Tuson got no further, at least under his own steam, than the French checkpoint at the English end of Eurotunnel. Yes, believe it or not, there is a piece of England, other than their embassy in Knightsbridge, wherein the French hold sway. Margaret Thatcher gave it to them in 1987 in return for a bit of the Eurotunnel terminal near Calais. The idea was to help control drug-smuggling and international terrorism but, quite frankly, had we received the whole of Calais in return I would still consider it a deal poorly struck.

Anyway, back to Henry, now being held in Folkestone by you kneau who.

Claude:	You have been dodging your military service with the glorious 43rd regiment in Lille.
Henry:	What are you talking about?
Claude:	You have a French mother and dual nationality.
Henry:	So what, I live in England.
Claude:	Aha, but you were born in France, Henri.
Henry:	I left France, I am told, when I was three months old and I haven't lived there since.
Claude:	Well, my little *déserteur*, you will shortly be residing there again.

Henry was taken from these shores under armed guard to the same grotty Citadelle in Lille where Sean Cornwell had recently been press-ganged. This time, though, they knew they had a bilingual on their hands. It took a whole day of high-level diplomatic wrangling to spring young Henry from the clutches of Générale Genocide, but were they sorry, did they apologize? *Non, non, non.* In the words of their embassy spokesman, Laurent Lemarchand, or Larry the Shopkeeper to you and me, "Mr Tuson had only himself to blame for his predicament. He could have been more careful and this would have been avoided. It is not as if French police will be parachuting into the heart of Britain to kidnap its citizens."

Just try it matey.

French Regional Poetry

From Gascogny, the cradle of Cyrano de Bergerac, we hear another rich, flamboyant voice, that of Emile Fortu. This from his 1761 epic "Sparks about my Helmet Fly."

> Oh, give to my loins
> That fathomless depth
> Wherein I might squander
> My Gascogny broth.
> Two jugs will I stand thee
> Of foaming champagne
> When you agree
> To have it off.

Chirac

Following the publication of the *I Hate the French Official Handbook*, a wave of despondency naturally enough swept over the country. From Montmartre To Marseilles rotten teeth were gnashed as wholesale feelings of inadequacy threatened to engulf Claude and the entire tribe of Gaul.

Despite the demolition of their culture, language and national identity, within two years the French somehow managed to pull themselves from this quagmire and had regrouped sufficiently to elect a new Président de la Republic.

The audacious upstart in question, the man who would dare to sit at the top table with the likes of Chancellor Kohl and Anthony Blair, was the former Mayor of Paris, whose principle claim to fame rested on his introduction of the motor-cycling pooper-scooper to the narrow streets of the French capital. His name Jacques Chirac.

President Chirac has worked long and hard at gaining a reputation for being something of a clown. Two years after becoming president he called a snap election for the National Assembly over a year before he needed to. The result was a huge shock with his bunch, the RPR and their right-wing allies, losing their 180-seat majority to the Socialists and their leader Lionel Jospin.

Chirac by all accounts is a man who likes to eat well and often. He typically enjoys three substantial meals per day, presumably to keep those masterful political antennae of his bristling away on all frequencies. Then again he may be trying to emulate the man he sees in Europe's driving seat, the man who matters, "Chancie" Kohl.

Ode to Chirac

A strange chap called President Chirac
Was well known for knocking the Kir back
He'd get a few belts in
With President Yeltsin
Then of comrades acknowledge the sheer lack

Menu

FOR A LIGHT LUNCH

for M. le Président Chirac
and his Guests from The Royal Society
for the Prevention of Cruelty to Animals

Pour Manger	*Pour Boire*
Les Amuses-Guelles	**Ch d'Yquem 1948**
Nichées d'Allouette	

Nests are made from halved and hollowed-out bread rolls, lined with *foie gras*, then stacked with soft-boiled larks' eggs and scattered with deep-fried larks' brains. The whole complemented by one of the great sweet white wines of all time.

Pour Commencer	**Rouge de Bouzy 1993**
Potage de Foie Gras Rouge	

A fine beetroot and red cabbage broth is decorated with floating islands of fine fat goose liver and sour cream. The wine is a light, but expensive Pinot Noir from the Champagne region.

Menu For A Light Lunch

Poisson   **Ch Grillet 1985**

Palais Elysée d'Homard

Balls of lobster and paté of force-fed goose liver are scattered on a
base of wilted spinach and covered with a pink sauce of grasshop-
pers crushed in double cream. To drink, the peach-blossom scented
white wine of the smallest appellation in the Northern Rhone, made
from grapes of the sensitive Viognier vine.

Bonne Bouche

Glace President

This unusual palate cleanser is made with a base of lemon-juice,
anisette and chopped bitter comfrey leaves frozen to an ice, covered with
a sauce of warm ducks' liver paté (goose-liver is too rich for this dish).

Entrée   **La Romanée 1961**

Boeuf a l'Ancienne Mode d'Angleterre

Ribs of beef are charred over an open fire, and served whole, and still
bleeding, with a bone-marrow sauce. The garnish of bread crusts
and watercress is in honour of the Count (sic) of Sandwich. The dish
is served with potato pancakes stuffed with *foie gras*. La Romanée is
a fabulous red burgundy, from a tiny vineyard, walled by the
Romans, and producing just 400 cases a year.

Fromages   **Ch Chasse-Spleen 1976**

On the board today we have some of the more unusually shaped French cheeses:

Rollot
Heart-shaped cheese from Picardy – soft, supple and tangy, like a good heart muscle should be.

Ramequin de l'agneau
Small cylinders of extremely hard goat's cheese (well, have you ever tried nibbling on a goat?), which are often used grated for fondue. Made in Bugey in SW France.

Tomme au Marc
Big wheel of cheese, fermented for six months in a vat of grape skins. Overpowering flavour and a smell to match – but don't take a lighted one near it!

Rocroi Cendre
Square block of cheese, ripened in wood ash. About the size and constitution of a small breeze-block. Their strong taste gets the Champenois all fizzed up.

Grand Murol

You have seen a doughnut, hein? This is the cheese to match. The pinkish-brown disc has a dinky little hole in the middle. Only the cowherds of the Auvergne know what it is for – but it does get very lonely out in the country. Supposed to be mild, if you can face eating it.

Venaco

This has escaped from Corsica – you can still see the marks of its wickerwork prison on the greyish surface. Has the smell of authentic Corsican goats and ewes.

Chateau Chasse-Spleen in Moulis is a good, but unclassified, Claret. In the words of Lord Byron "wine chases away the spleen" – not to mention the liver, kidneys and the other internal organs.

Dessert　　　　　　　　**Eau de Vie de Houx, G Miclo**

Tarte Fantasie de Strasbourg

An open tart of halved pears, rounded side up, in a *crème patissier* made with the local *alcool blanc* distilled from holly berries. When the pears are lifted out of the tart, it can be seen that they are stuffed with the best Alsace *foie gras*. The only fitting accompanying drink is more of the holly berry brandy.

Tea and herbal infusions will be available, but not coffee, as the Président has given it up for Lent. **Digestifs** will include authentic Napoleon Cognac and Nelson Rum, both distilled in 1801 and allegedly used (externally and posthumously) by their dedicatees.

Ode to Chirac

I'm President Chirac

I am I am

I'm President Chirac I am

I'm nobody else

There's only one me

I'm France Un

It's there on my airbus chérie

I'm President Chirac

Quite how is un miracle

I'm President Chirac I am and je suis

10 Things You Probably Didn't Know About Jacques Chirac

1. Jacques Chirac's real name is Dusty O'Hanlon
2. Chirac was voted European Brylcreem User of the Year, 1968
3. Although his wife Bernardette is a Roman Catholic, Jacques himself is a practising Zoroastrian
4. Jacques Chirac is allergic to pineapple and certain types of hairspray
5. On the only occasion Jacques Chirac used the Paris Métro he managed to catch his nose in the doors.
6. Jacques Chirac is a five-star member of the AA
7. Jacques Chirac has no sense of smell and only limited taste
8. Jacques Chirac was once all-comers roller-skating champion of Brittany
9. Jacques Chirac is a distant relative of Bill Owen, Compo in *Last of the Summer Wine*
10. Jacques Chirac was an extra in the 1959 film *Carry on Nurse*

Bonus fact: Jacques Chirac can only travel by helicopter when under sedation.

116

French Writer Seizes British Island For Patagonia

Writers have often been associated with romantic political causes. Byron in Greece, Hemingway and Orwell in Spain, but the claim of Patagonia to the 'Malvinas' islands is surely no business for a Frenchman, pen-pusher or otherwise to be inserting his nose into.

Even if the Patagonians have an indisputable claim on the Falklands, I just don't want to hear it from Monsieur Jean Raspail. So bugger off you meddlesome twerp and apply your energies into solving the very many pressing problems that beset your own neck of the woods.

Earlsfield Morning Messenger

March 19, 1998

Elspeth Jones, 43, a local woman was today behind bars in a French prison charged with reckless parking in a built-up area. "I had promised myself never to drive on the Continent again – after the last time," Ms Jones told the magistrate.

According to police, her car, a silver-blue Morgan 2+2, was parked over a metre from the curb and had already caused four accidents by the time she emerged from the pharmacy. "When she attempted to drive off, the situation rapidly deteriorated," said Inspector Auguste Darnell of the Boulogne gendarmerie.

I'm OK Euro K

So Wim Duisenberg is going to resign after four years as President of Eurobank so Jean-Claude Trichet can take over as Europe's Mister Money. *Non merci.* Because that's when we'll either be joining the Euro or the whole thing will be on the point of going belly up. Are the French going to run the Euro to suit them? Does pastis go cloudy when you add water?

tricher *.f.* (Act of) cheating. *Obtenir qch. à la t.,* to get something by trickery or fraud.

tricher *v.i. ƒ* tr. To cheat; to trick (s.o.).

tricherie *s.f.* Cheating (at cards, etc.); trickery.

tricheur, -euse 1.*a.* Given to cheating. 2.*s.* Cheat; trickster.

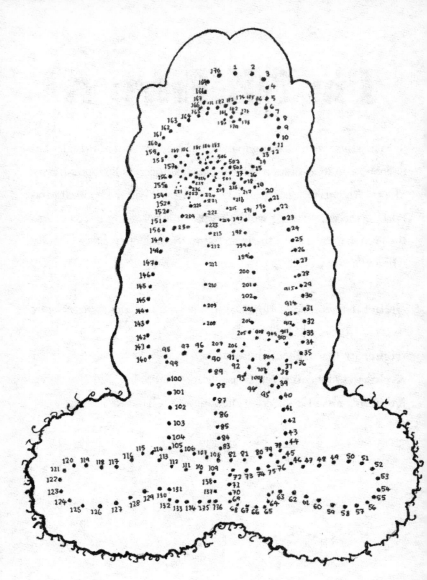

Join The Dots

The World Cup

Denise and I have it on the very best authority that during the so-called summer of 1998 there was a bit of a kick around footywise occurring in France. Unfortunately various colour-blind referees were allowed to muscle in on the act. Even worse, the "organizers" made the basic error of allowing the footballs – hand-stitched by FIFA-approved Chinese slave labour – to be filled with French air. While this may have worked wonders for the Frères Montgolfier, it did nothing whatsoever for practitioners of more ground-based pursuits.

If anyone has any further details, I'm sure the publishers of this book would be delighted to help you get in touch with your local branch of Sad Persons Anonymous.

Blasé

If the French aristocracy has a reputation for being a bunch of over-dressed poisoners, then one man who stands honourably aloof is Henri Julian Joseph Edouard Sylvestre 14ième Vicomte Cresselin et Duc de Blasé (1721–89).

Henri became more than a little famous for his phlegm, but then he did have an English mother to help stiffen his top lip. He fought his first duel at the age of 12 and, despite losing an arm, he insisted on going hunting three days later.

But if Blasé was blasé about physical pain, he cared not one fig for financial discomforts. When told by his creditors that he was bankrupt and would shortly be forfeiting all his land and possessions, he is said to have yawned and remarked "I'd better finish that *foie gras* then."

At the age of 56 he rode from Paris to Sicily to enjoy the favours of a young shepherdess on the strength of a sketch his valet had drawn. But when society beauties threw themselves all over him, as they did incessantly throughout his life, he would peer at them for a long moment through his monocle before muttering a simple "Oui" or "Non", with "Non" being the usual answer.

Henri Duc de Blasé was, according to all who encountered him, the most charming man they had ever met. He stood a little over 5 feet 4 inches in his usual outfit of Jade Imperial silk pyjamas – he wore them to the opera, on horseback, even in church. And yet he didn't seem to care about anything, at least about anything of any importance.

On the scaffold, waiting his turn for Madame la Guillotine, Blasé performed a tap dance and blew smoke rings to amuse the children.

10 Reasons Why We Might Not Always Wish To Lend France And Her People Our Unquestioning Support

1. Devil's Island

2. Charcuteries

3. Bathroom lights that only go on when you close the door

4. August

5. Suppressing the Albigensiens

6. "Birdcage Walk" along the Seine

7. Charles de Gaulle's revolving airport

8. French feta

9. The radioactive Pacific

10. "Breakfast"

Who Said It?

"Make no mistake about it, France is hell. Sheer unadulterated bloody purgatory. Do you realize that in the French we are dealing with a people who as recently as the 1790s decided it would be grand to have only 10 months in a year?"

a) U Thant, former UN Secretary General

b) Zoë Ball

c) Willy Brandt

d) President Dwight Eisenhower

e) William Burroughs

f) Prince Rainier of Monaco

g) Glenn Hoddle

* They all did.

126

A Visit From François

What's it like when the French come to stay? Are they over-awed, are they captivated, are they house-trained? For the following I am indebted to my neighbour, Belinda, a charmingly liberated example of English womanhood.

When François, a former boyfriend, got married, he decided to bring his young wife on a honeymoon to London and to stay with me in my smallish apartment in Fulham. I moved out into the sitting room, I filled their room with flowers and for 10 days I endured every possible disturbance such as their drunken attempts at breakfast-making at four in the morning. They trashed my room, ransacked my kitchen, contributed nothing whatever in the way of food or drink and when they finally left (with my keys) while I was out at work, they left no note.

When François rang six months later to tell me he was coming to London for a friend's wedding and to ask whether he and his wife could stay again, I told him I was busy and that I'd think about it. He rang back.

"It'll just be for one night ..."

"All right then."

The night before they were due, I was woken by my bell at 1.00am. It was them. They rapidly made themselves at home and were mortified when I declined their suggestion that we should revert to the same sleeping arrangements as during their first visit. At noon the next day when François surfaced, there was a smile on his lips.

"We've got a surprise for you, Belinda."

"Oh great." Could this be the overdue peace offering, I wondered, a case of fine champagne, a jewel, a work of art?

"Yes, we're staying for five nights."

* * *

Young Belinda, bless her, has experienced life on both sides of the Continental divide we sometimes call the English Channel. She was living once in a beautiful Parisian apartment, on the fourth floor to be exact. On the third floor were the building's oldest residents, a man and woman in their late seventies who made their presence felt on Belinda's arrival by banging loudly on their ceiling with a broom or somesuch.

"I thought they might need help," Belinda explained to me. "So I went downstairs and rang their bell only to be met with a torrent of violent hatred ... 'You young slut, how can we rest with your infernal noise above our heads ...' etc.

"Over the next weeks and months the couple embarked on a campaign of letter-writing – to my landlord, to the owners of the building, to the town hall and for all I know to the European Court of Justice. I could not flush my loo or break an egg without them thumping, swearing and denouncing me to some authority."

The situation resolved itself unexpectedly. Belinda was climbing up to her apartment one evening when she noticed Mr Angry sitting open-legged upon the staircase. In his lap was buried the head of a teenage rent boy.

"Bonsoir, monsieur," she called sweetly. And from that hour the banging, at least from downstairs, stopped.

Breather

Every so often when you're writing about the F-place and its denizens, you need to take a break. After 15 odd thousand words, Malcolm and I certainly do. We need to get away, as far away etc ...

"Have you ever made love listening to *Test Match Special?*" The speaker was Sir Adrian Hetherington, head of MI6 Counter-intelligence.

"I don't believe so."

"Come on man, don't shilly-shally about, have you or haven't you?"

"Well, once ... it was definitely the radio ... I was definitely ... the West Indies, final test at the Oval, yes, the answer is yes."

"Can you start Monday?"

The Heart Of The Matter

That's a whole lot better. Now, back to business.

Nothing perhaps exemplifies the Anglo-French dichotomy as well as an inspection of two superficially similar national pastimes, *boules* and bowls.

Both concern the release of an object from the hand towards a smaller object some distance away, the aim being to get as close as possible. Both call for a measure of skill, but here all similarities abruptly end.

They throw an etched ball-bearing, the size of an orange. We roll a subtly biased, grapefruit-sized "wood." They play on dirt, gravel or sand which they expect to be flattish. We roll upon bowling greens; levelled squares of pampered sea-washed turf, brushed, watered, spiked and kept in fine condition by a knowledgeable greenkeeper.

Bowls is an immensely cultured game, enjoyed for centuries by Britons of both sexes and all ages. It requires nerve, finesse, judgement and discipline. It is beautiful to both watch and play. Boules is an anytime, any place, Martini-like free-for-all. You could play in a prison exercise yard if they'd trust you with the big ball-bearings. It is an excuse to drink pastis on warm evenings and exclude oneself from female company.

When the French start playing bowls they will have taken a major step on the path to civilization.

The Gauntlet is Thrown

We, the authors, hereby issue a standing challenge to the *boule-chuckers* of the boulevards. Citizens of Paris, assemble a team of 12 of your finest *pétanquiers*, make your way to Maida Vale in London, home of the world-famous Paddington Bowls Club, and we undertake to administer to you, on the bowling green, the thrashing you so richly deserve. Paddington's legendary bowlers will then make the trip to Paris and sort you out at your own "game."

Saint Claude

Most European countries have their quota of barmy saints, but as in the present volume we happen to be dealing with the sons of Gaul, it is upon some of their more lurid candidates for canonization that we shall be focusing our spotlight. By way of an *hors d'oeuvre* I offer you St Sigismund of Burgundy; St Nicetius, about whom we learn, 'the extirpation of incestuous marriages caused him many difficulties' and St Remi who christened King Clovis – some say in cognac.

Never forget that for 70 years during the 14th century, the French hijacked the papacy from Rome and set up shop, or rather luxury department store, at Avignon. Now if it's a sainthood you'd be after, rubbing shoulders with God's number one earthling could just count in your favour. Accordingly you will not be surprised to learn that a number of rather rich and ambitious Frenchmen achieved sainthood at about this period.

Rather than retail the hagiographies of these credit card christians, let me tell you instead of St Gregory of Largres, the early health food fanatic. 'He ate barley bread, but that this might not be observed, he had wheat cakes piled on the table above his brown barley cakes. In like manner he drank form a dull glass goblet so that it might not be noticed he drank water while the others at his table were served with wine'!

Browsing for Frenchmen among the lives of the saints, one learns of St Ulphia who could stop frogs croaking; St Leobard who lived in a cave for 22 years and of St Rigobert, Archbishop of Rheims who got kicked out of town by Charles 'mine's a double' Martel and subsequently befriended a goose.

Finally, the big question, is there actually a St Claude? Well, as a matter of fact there is. In 1992 a French jesuit priest, Father Claude La Colombière was canonized some 300 years after his death. St Claude got the job of preacher to the Duchess of York and her husband the future King James II. Unfortunately he fell foul of some serious popish paranoia for which he was imprisoned and deported back to France a broken man.

Cherchez Le Patron

Who is the patron saint of France? Believe it or not, they've got four. In 1922 Pius XI declared the Blessed Virgin Mary to be the principal patron saint of the country with Joan of Arc achieving the silver medal position as the 'not quite so principal' patron. Because the BVM's chief feast day is that of her Assumption, when she is so frequently depicted flying through clouds, she was also in in 1952 made the patron saint of French pilots and aircrew.

Another patron saint of France, Paris and for good measure, headaches, is St Denis. He was sent from Italy in 250AD and preached with great effect to the Parisii on an inland in the Seine. Such was their gratitude they beheaded him at Montmartre but apparently the corpse rose to its feet, picked up its head and escorted by angels, walked the two miles to where the abbey of Saint Denis now stands.

French patron saint number four is Thérèse of Lisieux 1873–97, commonly known as 'the Little Flower.' She was one of four sisters to become Carmelite nuns, though whether she smoked Carmel Lites herself is not recorded.

10 Further Jewels Of The French Catholic Firmament

ST GENEVIÈVE – Saved Paris from Attila the Hun. (Where was she when Disney came to town?)

ST ODO OF CLUNY – Who 'combined the strictest discipline with a lively sense of fun.'

ST LOUIS – The only French king to have been canonized. Has spent the last 1,000 years trying to disprove the adage: 'No man is an island.'

ST SIDONIUS APOLINARIS – Country gentleman, poet, politician, son-in-law of Avitus (Roman Emperor), bishop and defender of Clermont-Ferrand against the Visigoths.

ST ROUX – 14th century healer. On his return from a pilgrimage to Rome, during which he had cured numerous plague victims, his family didn't recognize him and he died in prison, 'an imposter.'

ST RENÉ GOUPIL – Surgeon and jesuit lay missionary. Tomahawked in 1642 for making the sign of the cross on the head of a red indian child.

ST GERMAINE OF PIBRAC – Abused and scrofulous child with a withered hand, mocked by her neighbours as 'the little bigot' for her religious devotion. Produced spring flowers from her apron in mid-winter.

ST BERNADETTE SOUBRIROUS – But for this one there would be no Lourdes industry, for young Bernadette it was who saw the BVM and who spent the rest of her life having to tell people about it without revealing the secrets she was told.

ST GENESIUS OF ARLES (Not to be confused with St Genesius the comedian, I kid you not). This St G. worked as a court recorder and one day found himself being asked to transcribe an 'impious and sacrilegious edict' on the subject of christian persecution. Not only did he refuse the task, he flung down his registers at the feet of the judge and resigned from such a wicked occupation. For this act of rebellion he was beheaded.

ST AMADOUR – About whom nothing whatsoever is known but who is known nonetheless as 'the first hermit of Gaul.'

The Amazing French #4

DIDIER ST HONORÉ 1511–1563

To call Didier an aviator would be an exaggeration but yet, remarkably, he can claim to be the first Frenchman, and possibly the first human being, to attain flight. Didier St Honoré was a farmer, and on his farm he had a cow and a pig and some sheep. Now the winter of 1559 was an exceptionally hard one, particularly in the Massif Central which is where Didier and his large family happened to be. At night all the animals were happy to be herded indoors to find their place around the glowing hearth. Sleep cannot have come easily under these conditions. Imagine the wheezing of many children, the rumbling stomachs of the beasts. On the night of January 23, Didier could bear it no more. He crept out of bed and opened the trapdoor up to the loft where he kept a flagon of *eau de vie*. "Suddenly Claudette (the pig) broke wind in a truly deplorable fashion. There was a flash, a deafening noise and I was flying skywards astride my chair, my flagon on my lap." It is calculated that Didier was thrust to a height of over 625 feet before landing in a snow drift which his wife had nagged him to clear that very morning.

metamorphosis of the frog

Who Said It?

"The Cancan, Le Moulin Rouge, Les Folies Bergères, Toulouse Lautrec, La Belle Epoque, my arse. If ever there was a period in their history the French would do well to stop crowing about, it is the 1890s. Cholera, syphilis and absinthe: you could acquire them all in a single night and without even leaving your seat."

a) Winston Churchill

b) Henri de Toulouse-Lautrec, who added "I should know, I did"

c) Elspeth Jones

d) Ernest Hemingway

e) Eric Cantona

f) Thomas Crapper

Answer on page 126.

Bureaucratic Complications

France loves bureaucracy. The history of France is a history of *fonctionnaires* – no nonsense in France about civility or servant status. There are plenty of them, at European, national, regional, departmental, city and commune level. Most politicians have trained or served as civil servants, and seem to see it as their function to allow the civil service to continue in its accustomed form.

Monopoly

The basis for French bureaucracy is monopoly. The introduction of the Gabelle or Salt Tax during the Middle Ages made salt sellers into *fonctionnaires*: they were later granted the sole rights to sell tobacco and matches. As time passed, governments of all shades of opinion have seized the opportunity to monopolize anything new. Often, the technical innovation is made by an individual or firm, and then the government stops anyone else from doing the same thing. They do this in the name of efficiency, but it is really for convenience. The firm can charge whatever it likes. The workers – the *fonctionnaires* – have protected jobs. And who cares about the consumers?

In France, there is little competition. Gas, electricity, the railways, Air France and the telephone service remain nationalized, even though the EC commission has ruled that competition must be introduced. Water services are provided by commercial companies, but services and prices are controlled by the state. Half of the banking system is in public hands, and competition on interest rates and services is discouraged – mainly because the public half of the system is effectively bust. Even industries in sectors such as electronics, cars and aerospace are controlled by government fiat, and protected from competition.

What the government does not control, the trade unions do. Each political party has its trade union wing, so there is no force for reform. Unions control working hours (now the shortest in Europe), wages and employment – heaven forbid there should be any measures to improve efficiency that might lead to jobs being lost! Of course, with no innovation, and huge disincentives to sacking anyone, companies do not take on new staff. Late in 1997, the French unemployment rate was two and a half times that in the UK, with up to a quarter of young people being jobless.

Companies, workers and farmers expect the government to make up for the failures caused by the lack of market competition. They expect subsidies for everything – giving France one of the highest rates of government expenditure as a proportion of national income in the world. And what do these subsidies provide? More and more riots, demonstrations and manifestations as more people demand higher kickbacks.

But surely the French determination to modernize has paid off? The huge investment in nuclear power certainly helps to reduce global CO_2 emissions, so it should keep the Greens happier. And, yes, nuclear plants produce power that is cheaper than the coal-fired stations that they replaced. But the whole system is much too large for current demand, and the fall in the price of electricity generated from gas means that the nuclear power industry is returning nothing on its huge investment – hundreds of billions of Francs will have to be written off.

And what about the other *Grands Projets*? The TGV system is supposed to be the pride of the world. The trains certainly run fast and are very comfortable – mainly because so few people use them. The link from Paris through Northern France to the Channel Tunnel would break even if it carried 16 million passengers a year – not the 6 million that it now transports in a good year.

Do you remember Minitel? This put a computer terminal in every home, and was supposed to fight off the PC-based American threat to indigenous European technology. Initially it effectively replaced the telephone directory. Now, a decade or more later, it barely even does that.

We can go on listing examples, such as the French "investment" in Concorde and the Channel Tunnel itself, both of which dragged the British in, to their financial discomfort. They have tried to lead the world in fighter planes, solar power plants, rocketry ... They have gained some prestige, seen some terrible blunders, and lost even more money. But the only reason that companies would get involved was government pressure to conform, and an unstated (but understood) guarantee against losses.

Corruption

France is only notionally a democracy. There is an alternation of parties, but no change in policies. The political monopoly is compounded by the monopolies in goods and services. That breeds corruption: in a recent poll, 59 per cent of French citizens thought that most of their political leaders were corrupt. These monopolies effectively lie with the civil service, who can protect the other agents of the state against losses and liabilities.

This protective screen gives French officials and politicians the feeling that they can do what they like, where they like, so long as it is for the benefit of the French system. French foreign policy is run on an amoral basis. If it is good for France to supply arms to Rwanda, Iran or Iraq, then they will be supplied. International sanctions are an irritant, not a barrier. If the ministers of the importing country have to be bribed to buy French, then they will be bribed. If they have to intervene to keep the politicians that they have suborned in power, as in Rwanda in 1994 or perhaps in Iraq in 1998, they will. If a change of government or an international body such as Greenpeace gets in the way, then French forces are available to provide weapons, stage a coup or sink a *Rainbow Warrior*.

Sometimes, of course, the interventions are so blatant that the media find out. Then there may have to be some domestic or international enquiry. Not that this normally means that anyone will be punished. Between 1992 and 1997, hundreds of politicians were charged with corruption, including eight former ministers, two party leaders and dozens of MPs and senators. Robert Dumas, the president of the constitutional court, was charged with handling bribes worth 45 million francs – for a warship deal with Taiwan when he was Foreign Minister. Will he be imprisoned? Fat chance.

The press has started to report on French involvement in Rwanda. Senior army officers are said to have given details of how they armed the Hutu militia and so precipitated the massacres. The French are unwilling to fully participate in the war-crimes trials: protecting not only their own backs, but also being loyal to their allies.

Empire-building

The French are inveterate interveners in other peoples' business. They are always trying to run the affairs of foreign countries. The latest bureaucratic move in this game has been the expansion of *La Francophonie*. This was supposed to be a talking-shop for French speaking countries, a post-Imperial answer to the British Commonwealth. But where the French have a chance, they will try to control.

Remember back to the days of General de Gaulle, in Canada, declaring "Vive le Québec Libre". The Province of Quebec is a member of *La Francophonie*, although it isn't a country – yet. If it becomes one, let's hope it is more democratic than many of the members of *La Francophonie* in Africa. There are some odd new members of the organization, in countries with little historic connection to France, including Romania, with its new government which is nearly as democratic as that run by the Ceaucescus.

What is going to be the connecting link between all these countries? International Boules Test Matches? Or perhaps a network in which backs are mutually scratched, deals done, and the world is made safe for graduates of the Ecole National d'Administration?

10 Further French Things That Don't Immediately Endear Themselves To The English

1. Racism

2. The centime

3. Château Lafite 1784

4. The man who shot Nelson

5. Tea

6. Gastronomy

7. Le Mistral

8. Ski resorts

9. Post offices

10. Pigalle

French Regional Poetry

ALAIN CRUCIBLE 1934–89

From Lille, the tough northern industrial zone where the landscape is pimpled with slag heaps, we discover an uncompromising raw strain of Gallic Brutalism.

> *I breathe fire.*
> *My nostrils belch forth*
> *White hot girders*
> *Upon the thick disgusting smoke hell.*
>
> *Mad crashing thundering*
> *Squeals of metallic stress*
> *Cannon from the dripping walls*
> *Of my mind prison.*
>
> *And I haven't even*
> *Gone to work yet.*

The Amazing French #5

SEPTIME PARFAIT ET FAMILLE

Bonsoir mesdames, messieurs et bienvenue to my sonorous buttocks. Oui, je suis un petomâne. Je suis aussi the son of Le Petomâne. Bert I have neau need to speak with you in this conventionelle way ... Bbbrraaarrghghshshshbrrrroooooh, as we say in Clermont-Ferrand, the true home of French farting where the real voice of the people can always be heard.

And now I would very much like to perform for you a medley of popular airs et chansons. Let me just check if I'm in tune ... (We shall no longer attempt to transcribe Septime's lavatorial utterances. Once, we believe, was quite enough. If he does it again, expect to see a *.) ... a little sharp perhaps.

*. Ah, much better. You know a lot of people ask me if I eat a special diet, lots of beans or something. The answer is no, I go to the restaurant the same as everyone else, I like to eat bonne cuisine. I tell you any Frenchman can fart well if he puts his heart into it and has an ear for music. The music of the hemispheres we call it in Clermont Ferrand. **.

151

Oh, that reminds me of the farm where I grew up. Crowded with windy cattle. Some days you couldn't hear yourself think, let alone practice. *. My father was a magnificent farter. That was for you by the way, Papa. He farted all over France, all across Europe, he farted for the Tzar in St Petersburg, for which incidentally he was presented with a Fabergé egg studded with diamonds depicting the four winds. Strangely enough he would never perform in front of my mother, nor she in front of him.

Maman had won numerous local farting competitions as a teenager and she gladly seized the opportunity when Le Duc d'Auvergne offered to sponsor her to attend the National Trials. My mother was blessed with perfect pitch and she enjoyed a glittering international career, performing under the name of La Trompette. Many feel she could have farted for France for another 20 years had she not borne seven sons of whom I am the last. The Perfect Seventh she called me. *.

Anyway perhaps later I will tell you of the time she accompanied Nellie Melba in Waltzing Matilda. It is said that grown men, hard-bitten ranchers and prospectors, wept uncontrollably at the beauty of their duet. Right now it's on with the show so, let's rip *...

Ode to Napoleon

When campaigning the Emperor Napoleon

Was known to start drinking petroleum

For a nominal fee

He'd ignite his own pee

And perform with an outer Mongolian

French Regional Poetry

BLIND DRUNK

If there is a corner of France where they do not produce some distinctive alcoholic refreshment, then I have yet to find it. All over France people are distilling, fermenting, growing, harvesting and more with but one purpose to the forefront of their addled minds: to get resoundingly pissed.

Nowhere perhaps do they accomplish the task more full-bodiedly than in Cognac. Here you stand out if the end of your nose does not resemble a red golf ball. Children of primary school age find wine in their lunchboxes. In Cognac you are considered drunk only if you are unable to raise your glass. From this boozers' nirvana I offer you the verse of Marcel Rognon.

Night is day.

I toboggan just in my beret.

I kiss the autoroute and pray

Between the axles

As I crouch

The spray will stay away.

I dance

With my key

To the gendarmerie.

"Non. Eight helicopters will not suffice,"

I tell Paris.

I sing as I swim

In my empty pool.

Or is it

Yours?

Moi

10 Last Reasons For Having Serious Misgivings About Claude

1. Middle-aged men in tight trousers

2. Cardinal Richelieu

3. Klaus Barbie

4. Secularism

5. Steak tartare

6. The French Empire

7. Underwear advertisements

8. Flick knives

9. Marseilles

10. Poor joint rolling

Et Finalement...

So what, when all is said and done, IS a Frenchman? What does it all boil down to? Is there a fundamental difference of character between us and them or are we both just nations of euro-individuals.

Two words that spring to mind, I know not from where, are 'cock-sure' and 'bumptious.' In many important respects they're all a bit like Geoff Boycott. A Frenchman, by nature, seems to think he knows best and he is full of advice for the rest of mankind. Try getting him to shift his ground and a dozen arguments come flying at you, some highly emotional, others patently absurd. He has no use for pause or reflection because he instinctively understands the root of all problems just as surely as he knows their solutions.

On matters of taste he is equally immutable. There is one way only to study a Monet, open a bottle of wine or make *une omelette aux fines herbes* and there will only ever be one way. As well as being the fountain of all wisdom and the supreme arbiter of taste for the known universe, the Frenchman possesses another ineffable gift that will forever, at least in his own opinion, justify his exalted status: he has savoir-faire. He knows what to do, how to act and when to do it.

Let us all, I say, prostrate ourselves before his genius, let us bathe in the brilliance of his being. Let us worship, let us marvel, let us cease our stumbling about in the gloomy ignorance of our Albion, of our Britannia. Let each of us clasp the nearest Frenchman to our bosom and entreat him earnestly with the words, 'Please monsieur, help me, it has all been a terrible mistake, I want to be one of you!

When you don't have to try at all, try

ARROGANCE

Pour homme
      Pour femme
            Pour it down the sink for all we care

LA VRAIE ODEUR DE LA FRANCE